When Your Mother Calls You Home

Tracie Ball

When Your Mother Calls You Home
First Published in the United States of America
By Tracie Ball 2025

The events and conversations in this book have
been described to the best of the author's ability,
although some names and details have been changed
to protect the privacy of individuals

Ball, Tracie
When Your Mother Calls You Home
ISBN 979-8-9997919-5-5 (Hardcover)
ISBN 979-8-218-74674-2 (Paperback)
ISBN 979-8-9997919-0-0 (Ebook, Kindle Edition)

Cover design features the author's modification of the following artist's work in
the public domain:
"Sketchbook: Mountainous Landscape with Bridge"
Samuel Prout
(British, 1783–1852)
England, 19th Century
Graphite with Gray Wash
Original: 13.5 x 23.4 cm (5 5/16 x 9 3/16 in.)
A Gift to the Cleveland Museum of Art from Mr. and Mrs. Herbert N. Bier,
London 1954.648.f

Book and Cover Design by the Author
Edited by Quata D. Merit

For my younger self—
who endured and persevered, with faith in love and something greater.

For my friends, family, and mentors—
who have loved, encouraged, and supported every version of me.

For the Universe—
who trusted me to tell this story.

For you—
on the path with me.

∞

Have you considered that every event since the dawn of time unfolded in a Divine order so that when you arrived in this world at the right time, on the right date, in the right place—all of the people, experiences, and lessons intended for you could appear in your path exactly when they were meant to?

Introduction

If you have found this book, perhaps there is something in these pages meant for you. Maybe you are grieving, living with shame, recovering from trauma, or you might have lost your faith in something greater than yourself. Maybe you are missing connection, joy, or adventure in your life. Maybe you need to be reminded that there is magic waiting to be welcomed.

Whatever the reason this book has made its way to your hands, you are now part of this unfolding story because I have never crossed paths with another human being by accident. Every person I have met along the way had something to teach me or has served as a mirror for something I needed to see in myself. Connections strengthen us, and if there is one thing I hope every reader takes away from this book, it is that we are all connected in this beautiful world, which is full of magic if you allow it to appear.

The experiences I have documented in these pages have been reconstructed from memory, photographs, journal entries, workbooks, text messages, social media posts, and emails. I have tried to describe every event and interaction as accurately as possible.

As much as I wish I could introduce some of the people in these pages to the world, certain names have been changed to protect and preserve privacy. I have made every attempt to describe and portray people as I experienced them. Timelines may have been abbreviated out of necessity, but I took care to portray events contained herein accurately and factually.

This book represents two healing journeys for me. The first took place between February 7th and May 1st of 2024 after my life unraveled and I made the decision to leave my partner, travel alone from Ecuador to England, make a brief side trip to Italy, then proceed to India. The second journey offered deep healing, and took place during the nine months I spent writing and reflecting on my experiences in solitude. It was during the writing of this book that I did the work of integration. My work didn't stop when

I left India. In many ways, it was just beginning, and I am still feeling my way through the next chapter—with grace.

This book describes many traumatic and life-changing events, and I sincerely hope that I have given voice to my experiences in the service of love. If my story helps one person, the vulnerability required to share it will be worthwhile.

It's not perfect. On purpose.

The earliest manuscript feedback I received from a publisher was positive but suggested my first chapter felt "rushed," and the reader would benefit from a slower pace. I gave thought to this feedback and decided to leave the events as they happened because this is how I experienced the events. I wanted my life to slow down. I wanted a moment to breathe. But, as we all know, *pausing* is a luxury in the midst of tragedy or upheaval, so I decided to include you in that experience rather than make you more comfortable.

I also decided to let my writing reflect the state I was in as these events unfolded. There is a lot of crying in this writing because I was, in fact, doing a lot of crying. There was, perhaps, more magic unfolding than I had pages to convey.

Throughout this book, I have included dated entries that were recorded during my travels. The majority of these italicized entries are from my journals, which were never meant to be shared or read. Other entries might be verbatim-dated social media posts or workbook entries. I journal to order my thoughts. As you read these entries, you will witness the mess of my moments. You will be a party to my interior landscape—neurotic questioning, self-doubt or, at times, self-support.

This is not a complete accounting of all events during my three months of travel. However, these are the events that revealed where my heart had been directing me all along.

I hope you will enjoy the adventure through external and internal landscapes, and hopefully, find a crumb of meaning that is supportive in your own journey.

Where Do We Go From Here?

The trouble with being a feeling human is that inevitably, you will experience heartbreak. If you're lucky, you'll experience it more than once. There's really no pain like a broken heart and the feelings of grief that accompany it. That grief is the surest sign that love was present for a time, and, in my opinion, love is one of the only things worth knowing in this world. Of course, the greater the love, the greater the grief.

When it comes to love, I go all in. Some folks would rather not take chances with the odds, and they spend their entire lives with their hearts behind walls of stone. Anyone walking in my shoes might have shuttered their heart years ago and moved to the forest to live out their days as a hermit, but I am a seasoned professional. I experienced my first heartbreak shortly after I learned to walk, and since that time, I have consistently risked my heart over and over again, only to have it crushed, shattered, and barely beating at times. My greatest act of rebellion in this world is to continue to believe in love and to rise like a phoenix from the ashes with my heart shining outward despite my chances.

My experiences in relationships have run the gamut from two decades of, by most measures, a successful marriage to my son's father and in sharp contrast, a devastating experience with a presumed narcissist that spanned eight years and cost me almost everything. After the latter, I devoted nearly a year to therapy, recovery, and deep soul-searching solitude. Then, when I wasn't looking, I met André, and I was sure I had found *my person*.

André made every piece of the puzzle fall into place. He made sense of all my lessons, failures, quirks, strengths, longings, and dreams. He was everything I wasn't and everything I wanted. He made my wishes come true, and our cohabitation was effortless. I loved our simple rituals like cooking meals together or having coffee with the mountain sunrise. We worked hard, adventured, and laughed most days from morning to night. I could stare at him for hours, admiring the creases in his face, the way his beard came in, and the way light turned his eyes from brown to green. I loved the feel of him. The smell of him. The weight of him. I loved *him*. Unconditionally. I loved *us*. My love for him felt timeless, without beginning or end. Like I had always known him.

I wish I could tell you the number of times strangers approached us to say things like, "You two are so happy! It's inspiring," or, "You two are beautiful together," "You're glowing!" or, "Whatever you two have, I want." I could feel the beauty of our connection, and so could everyone around us. We had love. And it was magic.

Until it wasn't.

The price I paid for this love was living with the impacts of André's untreated mental illness. He didn't disclose this when we were dating or after we began cohabitating. He disclosed this after I experienced his temper and womanizing during what I would later understand was a manic cycle.

In the years prior to our meeting, he had been transparent about his struggles with "severe Bi-Polar Type 1" in the community. He publicly shared his diagnosis and gratitude for support and medical care. I can't say why he didn't disclose this early in our relationship. Maybe he thought he was healed, or it was in his past. Maybe he was afraid I would not love him if I knew.

Only he knows the answer.

The first time I experienced one of these phases, it was like a hurricane passed through my life and leveled everything. The peace of our home was disrupted by agitation that grew into anger and sometimes uncontrollable, unbridled, and terrifying rage. His love for me would disappear, and so would he. It was like he had been abducted, and an angry, loud, arrogant, womanizing stranger was left in his place.

During these episodes, which could last weeks to months, I was afraid of the man I loved. I often kept my opinions in my throat and shrank to keep the peace. The burden was heavy, and I would become depleted of energy, confused, and unable to make decisions. It wasn't just that my partner disappeared; it was that my entire life disappeared. I prayed intently for miracles and for the *real* André to be returned to me. It was hard to comprehend that this was the real André too.

These episodes came and went like a Category 5 Storm, and until I saw it for myself, I didn't fully understand the illness and the changes it could create in a person. The flirting, texting, interest in other women, and the plotting of affairs severely impacted my self-esteem, but these impacts are par for the course with the hyper-sexualization aspect of the illness. I was safe; then I wasn't. I was in a committed relationship; then I wasn't. I had a life plan and a partner; then I didn't.

It was during one of these painful cycles that I ended the relationship with André for the second time. His decision to forgo medication was a choice that had serious consequences for me. I could no longer live with his frightening temper, the ups and downs, or the impact on my self-esteem. I had done so much inner work prior to meeting him, and I wasn't going to self-sacrifice for a partner who wouldn't commit to self-care.

After a few months of a separation that really wasn't much of a separation at all, André suggested we see a counselor together, and he began a new course of treatment. The counselor provided communication tools that helped us better understand the forces at work in our relationship, and after a few sessions, we recommitted to each other. In the fourteen months that followed, we found our groove. For the most part, André's mood had stabilized; he didn't sweat the small stuff, and maintaining his health seemed manageable. Our relationship improved, and we began making long-term plans.

At the start of December, we set out on a four-month adventure that would give us the winter to live and work on a project in Ecuador, followed by a five-day stop in England, then on to India for a month-long yoga course in Rishikesh. André and I had been planning the trip to India since we met, but I had dreamed of traveling to India since I was a child. I was beyond excited for the plans in motion.

This was our second winter living in Ecuador, a small country in South America nestled between Columbia and Peru. The previous year, we designed and broke ground on a reforestation project along the river in the Quijos Valley, a biodiverse ecosystem where the Andean Highlands meet the Amazon rainforest. This season had been remarkably different than the last. Instead of spending our spare time exploring waterfalls or traveling by motorbike to other cities and regions, the country was in lockdown as the Ecuadorian government declared war with the drug cartels controlling the port cities of Guayaquil and Esmereldas. This largely quiet and peaceful nation had seen a sharp increase in gun violence, and multiple hostage situations and bombings throughout the country had resulted in a mandatory curfew. Anyone found in violation of curfew was arrested. Trucks loaded with military personnel armed with assault rifles circled the neighborhoods, and there were police traffic stops and inspections at all major intersections. People were glued to the television and genuinely fearful, which made me realize how accustomed I had become to America's gun violence. The realization added another layer to the sadness of the Western decline.

Meanwhile, in the rest of the world, war and tensions were on the rise. Russia's unprovoked invasion of Ukraine raged on, and Israel's bloody invasion of Gaza in retaliation for a terrorist attack perpetrated by Hamas was ongoing with thousands upon thousands dead. It was hard to reconcile terror and war when you were in one of the most beautiful, untouched places on earth. The butterflies and birds were completely unaware of the trouble. Water flowed without thinking about what was around the bend. Nature continued on, peacefully oblivious to our games.

The violence in the external world contributed to existential dread, and on February 2, a week ahead of the new moon, something happened that felt ominous and foreboding. It seemed to say: *Pay attention.*

André and I were having dinner on the terrace of a cafe when a torrential downpour started. The rain was so heavy and loud that we couldn't hear each other over the sound. Just as I was turning my attention from the landscape back to my meal, I heard a loud flapping of wings inside the restaurant and saw a large, dark mass flying toward my head. It took a moment to realize it was a huge bird, and it circled my head so low that I shrieked and ducked instinctively. It returned for a second pass at André's head, before flying into the empty restaurant and landing on a *¡Feliz Cumpleaños!* sign atop a long banquet table prepared for a party later that evening.

Happy Birthday.

The bird was a sickle-winged guan, about the size of a rooster, and it was the first I had seen there. These birds are mystically associated with rain, renewal, and fertility. In Eastern traditions, the guan is said to be a divine messenger that announces a spiritual quest. As I was leaving that evening, I noticed the bird had dropped a feather at my feet. I picked it up and tucked it into my jacket pocket.

Feathers are a gift from the Divine.

Maybe that bird did deliver an important message because five days later, my life was forever changed.

On February 7, unmedicated, André physically assaulted me in anger. The whole thing happened in the blink of an eye. I didn't see it coming, but also, I did. I knew this potential was in him. It's why I left the first time and the second. It's why one of my requirements was that he commit to mood-stabilizing treatment.

Before leaving on this trip, he failed to procure his medicine for the winter, and in the prior month, his symptoms had returned and slowly intensified. First agitation, then inflated ego, increasing volume, erratic driving, less sleep, more conflict, flirting with other women, and increasing anger. The morning of the assault, André got into a bit of a heated discussion with our landlord over lease negotiations. Within an hour, his anger was focused on our farmhand, and then, when there was no one else to blame, he turned his anger on me.

The whole morning I felt it coming. I began to make myself invisible, quiet, and prepared. I tried to soothe him. I tried to reason with him. Intuitively, I knew where this was heading—where this was always heading. André needed someone to be responsible for his feelings, which were big and out of control.

He reached his tipping point over something relatively benign —the wording of a message he asked me to write to a potential employee. He was very specific about how he wanted it worded. Giving it thought, I said, "Maybe you should write the message since your Spanish is better than mine." He raised his voice and began to pace and rant.

"Why can't you do anything I ask? Why does everything have to be an argument? Why does everything have to be a fight?"

I realized at that moment, he was projecting onto me how he felt about himself. I walked away from him, hoping he would self-calm, but he never self-calmed.

There was nothing like his anger. When he passed his red line, there was no turning back. His eyes would become wild, darting around quickly in all directions, and he often moved into my personal space, puffing up his chest, which was threatening and terrifying because I knew I was no match for his strength. As he continued to escalate, I could feel my heart begin to race. Because of the way he was pacing and circling, I felt like prey. My eyes filled with tears; my hands shook, and unfiltered words flowed from my mouth, words that were truthful but inflaming. Once I spoke them, they couldn't be unspoken.

"You are behaving like a child throwing a tantrum."

He leapt inches from my face and screamed, "You want to see a tantrum?"

I stood tall, looked him directly in the eyes, and prepared for what was about to happen. I didn't say a word. He grabbed me with force, pulled me to his chest with my palms pinned flat so I was immobilized, and then he threw himself backwards onto the bed, taking me with him while simultaneously wrapping his legs around me. We landed hard, me on top of him, and I had no way to catch myself. My neck snapped backwards, and he began squeezing his arms and legs around me tighter and tighter like a constrictor. I felt I couldn't breathe and started to cry, pleading with him, "Please let me go! I can't breathe!" while he screamed into my ear, *"HOW WOULD YOU FEEL IF I SAID THAT TO YOU?!?! HOW WOULD YOU FEEL IF I SAID THAT TO YOU?!?"*

He had some training in martial arts and knew how to inflict pain. He created so much compression around my ribs that I felt short of breath and panicked. With my entire body restrained, I had no way to break free or fight back except to sink my fingernails into his chest. When the pain of my nails became too much, or when he realized what he was doing, he released his legs, and pushed me up and off of him. Gripping and painfully twisting the flesh of my forearms, he plowed me into the cement wall using his shoulder and body weight to pin me. He applied pressure to the left side of my body while the right was smashed against the ungiving concrete. When he released my arms, he shoved me down the wall onto the floor, pushed into the tops of my shoulders, and held me there while screaming, *"YOU WANT TO KNOW WHY I WON'T MARRY YOU?!? THIS IS WHY I WON'T MARRY YOU!"* Then he left me there, crying on the floor for what felt like an eternity. It was enough time for me to realize everything I cherished was gone.

I thought for sure he would return and say, "Oh my God. What have I done? Are you OK? I don't know what came over me."

But he didn't return. I could hear the sound of video shorts playing on his phone in the adjacent guest room. My ears were ringing as I assessed the throbbing in my body. My neck felt strange, my wrists were burning, and my right shoulder ached. I felt my broken heart.

After the initial shock wore off, my mind began to busy itself, thinking of a way through the maze to the best possible outcome. I grew up in a home dominated by my emotionally unstable and violent father. I learned that once a man feels free to put his hands on you in anger, it won't stop. I thought about calling the police for help, but I wasn't certain of the protocol in Ecuador. Would authorities treat him with dignity because he was in crisis? Would he resist arrest and get shot? Tensions were high in the country. Would we both end up in jail? His handprints remained around my wrists, but surely I had left fingernail marks on his chest too. I didn't know the answers, nor was my Spanish fluent enough to provide a statement or navigate the legal process.

I composed myself and splashed cold water on my face. Then I spoke to him from the threshold of the guest room where he was relaxed on the bed, stretched out with ankles crossed, watching videos on his phone like nothing had happened. He exuded an eerie calm. Before I could tell him my plan, he looked up at me and said, "You're fucking crazy. You are fucking crazy. I was just trying to hug you. Look what you did. You scratched me with your nails. *YOU SCRATCHED ME WITH YOUR NAILS!*"

I was completely stunned. He was raging moments earlier, had assaulted me, and now he was blaming me for hurting him. *Just trying to hug me?!?* But then, I had a moment of clarity. In the past during these phases when André did something shameful, he would *double down*. He would say or do things that would inflict

16

more harm. He seemed to want my pain to be *deeper*. He wasn't going to give me the comfort of an apology or validation. He wasn't going to be bad or wrong. He was creating a victim's story that made me responsible for his pain, actions, and aggression.

I stood there for a moment thinking: *This is why you won't marry me? No, this is why I won't marry you. This is why I left you in the past. This is the ugliness that shows up because you don't take care of yourself. It's only getting worse.*

I felt a moment of calm in the eye of the storm and knew what I needed to do for myself. I looked at the stranger in front of me and said, "I'm leaving."

I felt afraid, but I also knew what was right. I worked quickly, stuffing most of my belongings into my bags, called a taxi, and waited at the curb for the driver who would take me to a hostel in Baeza, the largest town between the farm and Quito. I really didn't know what *leaving* meant. André and I were traveling abroad with more than a month of plans ahead of us. Our flight to London was set to depart in less than two weeks. And, back in the United States, we were living together. All I really knew at that moment was, *I needed to make myself safe.*

Climbing into the backseat of a yellow taxi in the haze of a post morning rain and pulling away from the house was one of the most surreal moments in my life. Every second lasted minutes. Every detail and breath took place in a pause.

I made the decision to leave. I chose myself.

When I arrived at Casa de Rodrigo, its namesake owner greeted me at the gate.

"Tracie! What are you doing here?"

I had several interactions with Rodrigo over the past two years, and I knew him to be a good, trustworthy, family man who ran a quiet, respectable establishment. The moment we made eye contact, my own eyes filled with enough water to drown us both.

He gave a nod and said, "OK, let's get you a room."

17

I appreciated that I didn't need to explain myself. I didn't need to talk about it. I was grateful in that moment for people who could intuit without words. People who recognized deep pain and offered safe harbor.

Rodrigo showed me to my room, which was tidy and smelled like freshly laundered linens. There was something comforting about the scent. It reminded me of my grandparents' home, my childhood safe place, a home that was always cared for, clean, and tended to. There were two beds in the room with a nightstand between them. There was a walk-in closet, which was unusually generous for Ecuador, and a private bathroom with hot water *and* water pressure. The combination of hot water and pressure was a rarity in this country, as far as I could tell. I had been able to find hot water and *no pressure* or pressure and *no hot water. This* was a luxury.

"*Es perfecto. Gracias.*" (It's perfect. Thank you.)

Rodrigo, who was awaiting my approval on the other side of the threshold, looked proud and in English said, "OK, Tracie, let us know if you need anything." He lowered his eyes, bowed his head a bit, and pulled the door closed as he left the room.

I walked over to the heavy wooden door, turned the lock, drew the curtains, climbed into bed, curled into a ball, and cried.

The hours passed like years without a thought for food or sleep. My mind and heart raced all night long. I felt such deep anguish, and I wanted to not feel it. The thing about heavy feelings like grief and despair is that when you're feeling them, it seems as though they will never end. And that's how I felt, but I knew the fastest way to heal it was to feel it. So I committed to feeling it. *All of it.*

I found myself in that familiar state once more—a pile of ash. Only, this time, it felt different. This time, I felt alone and without hope. In some moments, I had the wherewithal to remind myself that I had been lost in this wilderness before and that even the smallest amount of faith could, eventually, help me find my way out, but it was too soon to believe it.

I occasionally left the bed and moved my crying operation to the shower, so I could let the hot water soothe the stiffness of my neck and body. The red handprints around my forearms had faded, and in the silence and calm of that little room, I was beginning to experience small clearings in the fog, but I was not yet able to make sense of the event that brought me to the place. I thought of calling my mother, my friends, or family, but I dreaded sharing the news that for the third time in my adult life, a long-term relationship I had given my whole heart to had fallen apart. My shame was preventing me from reaching out for the lifeline I needed.

When my friends and family last saw me in early December, I was a happy, confident woman with a vision and a mission. A little more than two months later, I was a traumatized, frightened woman, alone in a foreign country without a plan. I felt vulnerable in every way. I needed to talk to someone, but I wasn't ready to reach out for support. So, I decided to talk to myself. I sifted through my bag and found my leather-bound journal and a pen; then I settled into a nest of pillows. In no time, I had filled ten pages. This act of writing and giving voice to my pain seemed to lessen it.

February 8
I have barely moved since arriving in this room yesterday. My eyes were fixed on the pitch-black ceiling all night until the first morning light began to define the shape of the fan and fixtures I had been staring at for a dozen hours. I feel ashamed of my string of failed relationships, and I have been thinking almost obsessively about André since I left. I left him in crisis. But was he? Was he experiencing an episode, or is he violent? Would he find me here and do something worse? Does he love me? Was any of it ever real? How could someone hurt a person they love? My mind is filled with

questions, memories, and observations, trying to solve the problem, trying to make sense of what happened, and I feel panic. What if he harms himself? What if he harms someone else and is imprisoned? My inner dialogue informs what I need to admit, that I feel responsible for the feelings, actions, and mental health of others. I think, "If he harms himself, it's my fault. If he harms someone else, it's my fault. I left him alone in a foreign country."

What if I cared for myself like I care for others?

I can hear guests shuffling in the hall. It's such a waste to be self-confined to a hostel room working through the pain of heartbreak in one of the most beautiful and biodiverse places in the world. Why did this have to happen here? Now? Why not at home? If I continue on this trip, I have ten days until my departing flight. Ten days to get my shit together. I need to get clear, focused, and come up with a plan, but at present, I feel lost, directionless, and alone. I'm so far from my family and friends. André is my life partner, professional partner, best friend, lover, and confidant. Now all those roles are vacant at once. The implications are heavy with one looming question. Do I keep my travel plans or return home? Do I have the courage to complete the remainder of this trip alone? Can I enjoy this dream trip despite the dramatic change in circumstances? The thought of traveling alone overseas is triggering, and the thought of traveling alone through India is overwhelming. Women have accomplished far more adventurous solo trips than this though. I have a friend who traversed the Himalayas alone long before cell phones, GPS mapping, and translation apps. I recently met Darcy Gaechter, who successfully paddled the Amazon River from source to sea alone and documented her journey in her book Amazon Woman. I imagine her asking me why I'm afraid to board a commercial flight with a fully stocked bar and stay in a hotel in a developed country. I ask myself, what would Amelia Earhart do? Several life experiences taught me to fear being alone as a woman in this world. I had a sense of safety traveling with a man that I didn't have as a single woman, and the irony of that is not lost on me. The person who provided the illusion of safety was the one who harmed me. The cut is deeper when you are harmed by someone you love and trust. Someone who should protect you. And this is also a recurring theme in my life.

When I really examine who I am in relationships, I give everything. I go all in and invest in shared dreams. I over-give. I am naive when it comes to love. I think my partner feels and loves like I do. I think they are honest because I am honest. I think they are committed because I am. I think they feel the love and sacredness I feel. The lesson I have yet to learn is that love is my experience. I am the creator and source of the love I feel. It is not outside me. Could I generate this feeling on my own without a partner? Can I love myself the way I love others? I saw my reflection in the mirror earlier and noticed my appearance is ashy and sad. My eyes are puffy from crying; my neck still aches; and my vibrancy is gone. I thought to myself, "Is this someone with self-love and self-respect?"

* * *

I was startled by a knock and cringed because I had seen myself in the mirror. I pulled myself together and opened the door to find Alexandra, Rodrigo's wife, smiling. She graciously invited me to join her family for breakfast.

"*No, todo bien, gracias. Quiero estar solo.*" (I'm all good, thank you. I want to be alone.)

She looked at me with the softest eyes and knowing expression; her brows lifted a little in the center, and she said, "Tracie, you have to eat, or you will get sick."

This caused me to realize I hadn't eaten in over twenty-four hours, and right there, in front of me like a gift, was someone offering kindness. I softened, thanked her for the invitation, and followed her to the dining room where Rodrigo and their two sons greeted me.

Alexandra was a sophisticated woman who had traveled abroad and had impeccable taste. She dressed well; her home was filled with meaningful objects that conveyed authenticity instead of opulence; and it was apparent that she genuinely loved her family. I'd bet her astrological sign was Taurus, like mine. She was a natural caretaker who had created a zone of domestic bliss, free from the outside world. An impressive collection of happy plants in the courtyard served as a testament to her care. Hospitality was the perfect work for her.

She made an Italian espresso, which was a rarity in the land of instant coffee, and the smell alone cleared some of my mental haze. She had also prepared a complete breakfast of eggs, fruit, pastries, and bacon. At the sight of it, I realized I was hungrier than I thought and grateful for this comfort. We exchanged awkward, pleasant conversation about the weather and upcoming festivals, and she included every proud Ecuadorian's favorite question, "*Te gusta* Ecuador?" Only this time, when I was asked how I liked the country, my eyes filled with tears as I said, "*Si, me encanta.*" (*Yes, I love it.*)

Tears were apparently Rodrigo's cue to take their two children off to school, and after hurried goodbyes, Alexandra and I found ourselves in the sacred space of *woman-to-woman*. After a few moments of awkward silence, Alexandra asked the dreaded question, "*¿Esta todo bien, Tracie?*"

My bottom lip quivered because I was about to tell a lie or the truth. The truth felt too painful to share. I tried to explain my situation in a string of broken Spanish. My comprehension of the language was very good, but my ability to speak was a struggle. I knew what I wanted to say, but it took a while to organize the sentence in my mind and send the message to my mouth. My skill with the language was still that of a toddler navigating the world with basic phrases but good manners. *Yes. No. I want. I need. I like. Please. Thank you.* I didn't know how to describe the complexity of *why* I was there in her hostel and not with my partner in the home we had rented. Or why during breakfast an occasional stray tear made its way down my cheek.

I pardoned myself for a moment and typed a paragraph of text into the translation app on my phone. I handed it to her, so she could read the text in Spanish. As she read my words, I realized she may be shocked to learn I could formulate complex thoughts and ideas into conversation.

She turned her eyes back to mine, her shoulders sank, and she said, *"Lo siento."*

Lo siento is a phrase that is the equivalent of "I'm sorry" in English, but it actually means *I feel it*. And that is what her eyes, expression, and melting posture conveyed. *I know this pain.* It's truly amazing what happens when two people create a bridge through empathy. We continued our conversation through translation and broken phrases, and I felt grateful for this technology and the sudden sisterhood we had found in that moment. I thanked her for her kindness and generosity, and I hugged her before returning to my room, bettered by our connection.

February 8
One of the things I need to remember—and I mean really remember —is how the Universe cares for me when I'm in need. How people show up for me. I think I have an authoritarian mindset imprinted in my Christian Protestant youth that believes things happen to me because I am being punished for sin. What if the Universe is loving and supportive, and I'm being given the opportunity for something more aligned with who I am? What if it's not a punishment but a redirection? What if it's a lesson, a blessing, or both? What if I focus on what shows up for me right now and not what I've lost?

* * *

I settled into my room, opened my laptop, and located journal prompts from a Jungian shadow work class I had taken and began to explore my feelings and relationship patterns through writing. *When did this type of relationship first show up in my life? When did it repeat? What do I tell myself about it? What part of myself do I deny?* As I contemplated this, I received a notification of an online meeting beginning in fifteen minutes. I looked at the calendar and saw that I was scheduled to participate in a ceremony with one of my mentors, Manari Ushigua, a traditional healer and the spiritual leader of the Sapara Nation in the Ecuadorian Amazon. I considered bailing on the event because I wasn't sure I could focus and be present. But also, I figured I should trust the timing.

I felt a deep connection with Ecuador and its people. I was pulled to the place, in the way I felt the pull to India that started long before meeting André, a pull from the knowing of my heart.

Several years ago, during the pandemic, I was feeling called to explore my purpose after a series of life-changing events had brought me to a more profound understanding of healing, connectedness, and spirituality.

I became somewhat obsessed with the idea that everything in the natural world has the potential to heal us. Rocks, minerals, trees, animals, plants, earth, air, and water have medicinal properties that are revered in ancient healing traditions like Ayurveda, traditional Chinese medicine, herbalism, and shamanism; yet most of the modernized world is far removed from nature, its wisdom, and its healing benefits. The modern world is connected via Wi-Fi, Bluetooth, broadband, and satellite, but it is no longer connected to the Universal energy that vibrates through every living thing on this planet. Call it what you like, but that energy is at the heart of every ancient religion and healing practice.

My curiosity around this idea, that everything natural is alive with energy and has the potential to contribute to our survival or healing, was growing and expanding, and I imagined not only

24

incorporating natural elements into healing work but also using my privilege to protect wild places and indigenous lands and to serve the planet through reforestation and restoration efforts. I was reading book after book on these subjects and enrolled in several courses and workshops to learn everything I could, but there was something else happening during this time that wasn't easy to understand or easy to explain. I was having unusual encounters with animals.

This started out with animals showing up around my house. An owl perched on the same limb of a tree outside my window, on the exact same day two years in a row and no other day. Deer began to walk right up to my home's windows and press their noses to the glass, peering inside. They began to approach me while I was gardening and let me pet them or feed them apples. A red fox with an infected leg wound came to me to die on the exact day my grandmother was dying from an infection in her leg. An adorable field mouse crept up to me in the kitchen, stopped and stared at me. When I picked it up, it died in my hands.

Once, I heard a shuffling noise coming from the basement, and I was a bit nervous because I was living alone, but I went down the old wooden stairs to investigate and found a small box marked, "Buddha." The box was shaking. I thought for sure I was going to find a rat inside. I took the box outside and opened it, and inside was a baby opossum with its prehensile tail wrapped around the arm of a Buddha statue. I have no idea how the little creature got into the house or up the side of the shelf and into the box, but it did. Butterflies began landing on me regularly; a hawk started perching on the fence outside the window every time I was working, and a huge two-foot tall female red-tailed hawk visited almost every day, flying low over my head whenever I mowed the grass. I was also seeing animals in my meditations and dreams and so, I felt I needed a teacher who could help me understand what was at work in my life.

In late summer of 2020, I was standing outside, barefoot in the grass, staring up at the moon, and I said a prayer aloud, "Please bring me a teacher." I swear, seconds later, I received a text message from Maria, a friend from Colombia. She was standing barefoot on the beach admiring the moon from her corner of the globe, and I laughed at the synchronicity. *I was standing barefoot on the earth, admiring the moon too!*

We caught up a little bit, and I told her of my recent interest in natural healing methods and my desire to find a teacher. Our conversation reminded her of a physician friend of hers in Ecuador who practiced medicine alongside Shamanic practitioners.

As evidence that speaking a wish creates magic, in less than a week, I was meeting Manari Ushigua through the technology of video chat with an interpreter. My first meeting with him was equal parts awkward and charming.

Neither of us were technologically inclined, and the sight of this beautiful, brown-skinned man with broad, flat cheekbones, glossy black hair that fell to his shoulders, and a crown of glorious colorful feathers on his head is not who I imagined I would be speaking with when I finally adopted use of this technology. But, there I was, speaking to a medicine man in a remote village of the Amazonian jungle of Ecuador through the miracle of technology.

September 3, 2020
During our conversation, Manari explained the Sapara people were severely impacted by the pandemic, and he expressed concern that the knowledge and songs of his people, passed down in the oral tradition, and the Amazonian jungle itself could disappear if he did not share nature's messages with the rest of the world. So he was doing just that. He has enlisted a group of volunteers to assist him in this quest, using technology to expand his reach and social media to amplify his voice. We discussed my pull to Ecuador, my connection to nature, and my spiritual path. I told him of my encounters with animals and

specifically, the animals that were appearing in my meditations and dreams like a confronting black jaguar.

Manari advised, "You must come to Ecuador as soon as you are able. You are ready to connect to all the spirits. This is why all the animals are coming to you, and in your visions, meditations, and dreams. They are ready to connect to you because you are open. In Shamanism, there are two things animals teach you. One is the way of life, and one is the way of death. One is life-giving and the other is letting go. The jaguar that is coming to you in your dreams is the voice of the spiritual world, and it is trying to reach you to give you your purpose. The jaguar can teach you life-giving and letting go.

"The animals that are coming to you are also your guides. They are showing you the way, so you can begin learning and use plants to heal. Animals represent spirits in the spirit world. The spirit world is helping to bring information on medicinal plants to you. Any time you start working with plant medicine or any spiritual path you choose, it is important to remain humble. Work from the heart, not the ego. Through meditation or visualization, the plant will tell you how it would like to work through you.

"We do not need technology to connect. If you need any recommendations or help, you can connect with me directly in dreams or the spirit world because you have the ability to do this.

"Last night, I felt your spirit. [I acknowledged that I had seen him in my dream the night before.] Once I saw you today, I remembered the dream about you last night. We were standing side by side, looking over a very big river. You were just standing next to me, not speaking. Then you turned into a small ball, and I took you in my hands and put you in a smaller river in the rainforest . . . in the Amazon. I said, 'I'm going to take you to a smaller river with a lot of fish.' We were standing in the small river with a lot of fish, and there were many trees. A lot of trees. The world is going to become like the trees. The houses will be built in the trees, not outside the trees. But this is not a dream. The future is going to be related to the trees and

animals. And I realized I had this dream because I was going to meet you today. You are going to teach people to live in the trees."

* * *

Since my first meeting with Manari, I have spent nearly eight months in Ecuador restoring commercial cow pasture to native food forest while documenting my learning curve. Manari is now reaching a wider audience and sharing his meditations and teachings online, and he has also created a healing retreat on his ancestral lands.

February 8
The healing ceremony Manari shared today began with meditation, prayer, and sacred song to connect to the Spirit of Love. Because the Spirit of Love is exactly what I need at this moment, I joined. Manari asked participants to accompany him in a meditative state while he used a rattle to accompany his singing of sacred, ancient prayer songs to invoke the Spirit of the Boa to assist us with our connection to the Spirit of Love. Ten minutes in, I was enjoying a deeply relaxed state of blissful super-presence. My mind was sharp and clear. I reached that beautiful space of awareness that transcends the thoughts of the mind and sensations of the body. In my mind's eye, I began to see clearly a massive boa in front of me. It was moving out of the dark nothingness toward me, into my heartspace. I felt it energetically wrapping and turning around my heart, moving up through my throat, and finally exiting my mouth. It felt as though this spiritual, energetic snake was dislodging centuries of stuck words, emotions, and stories. I was getting flashes of times in my life when I had suffered in silence, and I connected with my desire to free myself of this pattern so I could allow my womanhood, emotions, ideas, creativity, expression, and feelings to flow freely. I wanted my voice to be set free. I began to experience myself in another lifetime. I was

perhaps a Bedouin, a nomadic desert dweller, and I felt powerless because I was a woman. I hated my life. I was always moving and yet I felt imprisoned. I was full of ideas and dreams, but I was nothing more than property. I was on my knees with full skirts falling around me. My head was covered, and I wore many jewels on my wrists and at my temples. I felt hopeless, and I was weeping into a well, feeling as though I had been punched in the gut. My sense was that my husband punched me in the stomach. Something about this, whether memory or a story created by my imagination, is aligned with how I am feeling right now. It resonates: the constant shifting plans and moving, the powerlessness in the face of male anger, the experience of her. I need to be living the life that she dreamed of. I need to liberate her. I need to fully embrace my freedom and stop procrastinating and derailing my dreams.

* * *

Did I have a past life? It was all like a memory. Well, except for the snake part. I felt stunned by this brief experience with Manari and expressed gratitude to him for sharing his gifts. After the ceremony ended, I closed my laptop and my eyes.

Manari helped bring peace over me, which allowed me a brief sleep. I awoke around noon, ready to leave my room. I needed sunlight, movement, and coffee. A quick face check in the mirror revealed my eyes were looking less puffy and almost normal. I decided I could walk down the street without anyone asking *"¿Estas triste?"* (Are you sad?) because in Ecuador, my business was everyone's business.

From the moment I left my room to my first step onto the street, I felt as though I was just learning to walk my body. It was as if I was a driver in an awkward machine and hadn't quite mastered the controls. I was *making* my body walk against its will because it would rather be alone in my room. I pushed against the feeling, and

29

the farther I walked in the sun, the lighter my body seemed to be. I still felt alone and vulnerable even though this was a quiet little town not impacted by the violence taking place in other parts of the country. These streets were usually buzzing with activity, but there was no one on this two-block stretch of village, just me and a lonely mule saddled with milking jugs tied to a post.

I turned the corner and reached the coffee shop only to discover it was closed. I felt a little dejected since walking to buy a coffee was my first goal since starting my life over ten minutes ago, and it didn't work out as planned. It was the only cafe in town, so I turned back toward the hostel, and about a block from where I started, I heard "Tracie!" from a balcony above the street. I looked up to see my friend Paulo, an English-speaking Ecuadorian who intermittently lives in the states.

"Want to come up for coffee? I just got a new machine."

I cannot believe this luck! Seriously?

Moments later, he unlocked the door at the street; I followed him up the stairs, and he gave me a tour of his beautiful new home.

I sat down at his kitchen counter while he went to work making the finest cappuccino I had experienced in Ecuador. He took care with every step, grinding coffee beans from his friend's nearby farm and texturing the local milk to the perfect temperature. I loved his demonstration of care and pride.

Over coffee, we talked about conservation, and he shared dozens of photos of land he had recently purchased near the border of Colombia. His eyes lit up as he described the place and riding his horse there. It was beautiful to witness people aligning with what brought them joy or fed their soul.

It was a lovely visit, and I thanked him for the coffee. Silently, I thanked him for not asking why I was traveling without my partner. He didn't ask about André once. And again, the Universe showed up for me. A cup of coffee might not seem like the kind of prayer the Creator can be bothered with, but something was working magic behind the scenes, and not only had I run into a friendly face, but I had also been gifted with the perfect cup of coffee.

I stepped out onto the sun-washed streets and was once again present to the emptiness of this usually bustling town. I too felt empty as a result of violence. *Is it worth having dreams in this world?* My deepest desire was to make a difference with what remained of my life. I'd reached an age that was a fulcrum point where all my knowledge, experience, failures, successes, and relationships could inform something meaningful in this world, and I was eager to manifest my vision. I'd been allowing life to flow and unfold for almost four years, developing my idea for a non-profit education and retreat center devoted to healing people and the planet. It was equal parts exciting and daunting. When I felt overwhelmed by the scale of my dream, self-doubt crept in.

Have you ever had an idea so big that you didn't know how it was going to come together, but you could feel its existence in the future? I knew I'd get there; I could see it, but I didn't know *how I'd get there.* And then, it occurred to me . . . I wasn't done healing. This experience was uncovering something I had missed.

February 8
What I am experiencing right now is a shift in my self-awareness, revealing what it is at my core that is preventing me from playing large. I was programmed with messages of "not good enough" and unworthiness as a child, but those were the projections of the unhealed onto me. I have accomplished great feats already, but twice I have placed all of my focus and energy on the care of a man who won't or can't care for himself. What is this pattern? I see it. I am trying to earn love or be good enough through acts of service. I am giving my time, energy, and money to someone who doesn't mirror back to me the love and compassion I give. And as long as I am stuck in this energetic loop, I will not give my dream the attention it requires.

Why try to build this dream with someone who is incapable of consistency and has no regard for my well-being? I can build it on my own. If I commit to myself and to serving the greater good, the Universe will unfold in my favor.

* * *

February 9

I fell asleep around midnight, and around 1 a.m., on this day of the New Moon in Aquarius—which is purported to bring a shift in my sign of Taurus—I awoke to what sounded like a bat inches from my head . . . so near the headboard I could feel its wings disturbing the air. I bolted out of bed and ran to the light switch. On the headboard was a giant, female, black witch moth. I have no idea how it got in. It flew toward the ceiling light and seemed content there, so I crawled into bed and pulled the covers over my head. This morning, I captured the moth, which was as wide as both my hands flat, and released it through the window. After my experience with the guan, I was curious if there was lore associated with this bat-like creature. This moth is referred to as "mariposa de la muerte," or the butterfly of death. It is said to be the bringer of death. Farther north in Colombia, legend holds it is the earthbound spirit of a witch, enchantress, or sorceress. For a moment, I considered it might be an omen that André was going to die. I couldn't fathom that the last moment we spent together would mark the end of one of the most important and growth-filled relationships of my life. He has not reached out since I left. There has been no contact. No apology. I don't know what is next, but I do know who is dying. It's me.

After checking email this morning, just as I was closing my computer, I noticed a daily headline from Parade magazine: "The New Moon in Aquarius Says You Can Buy Yourself Flowers."

* * *

I joined Alexandra for coffee, and once again, she made a hearty breakfast. She informed me I would be joining her every morning. We spent an hour talking about life, and she shared with me that a neighboring hostel referred to their establishment as *Ohio*.

She asked innocently, "What does that mean?"

I said, "I was born and raised in Ohio! It's a state in the United States not known for excitement. It doesn't have mountains, whitewater, volcanoes or animal predators. It's fairly safe from natural disasters, so it's affordable and the people are nice."

She shifted to amusement. "Ohio is a compliment!"

I told her the next time I return, I'd bring her an Ohio flag. It was the first time I had laughed in a while. I was grateful for her presence and for the safety of her home where I could be my introverted self and process grief in *my* way.

I returned to my room, made a nest of pillows in the bed, then curled up with pen and paper and started excavating every romantic relationship that brought me to this moment. I examined all my experiences with love—the good, the bad, and the ugly. Memories surfaced and words poured out of me for hours and hours. I went through the ink of two pens and had a few deep realizations. I recalled my first love, a sixteen-year-old football star who cheated on me with a girl who had something he wanted in a girlfriend—big breasts. At fifteen, mine hadn't yet arrived, and as a matter of fact, whether they ever did is debatable. I wanted love and acceptance, but what I got from this world was a constant stream of messages about the inadequacy of my body, my worth, and my place as a woman.

During my sophomore year of high school, I met Kevin, and I fell hard in the way teenagers do. He was beautiful, like an Adonis. He was smart, funny, had close friends, loved his mother, and genuinely loved me, I think; as genuinely as a teenager can love someone. He was two years older than me, and after he graduated from high school, he attended university about an hour away, which created physical distance between us and, truthfully, that created longing. He began to talk about long-term commitment.

So, here was a boy growing into a man who had every quality I wanted, so you know what I did? I sabotaged the relationship because I didn't feel worthy of his love and kindness. I didn't realize it at the time; it wasn't conscious, but I broke up with him, and then I felt tremendous pain when he moved on and met someone else. He isn't *the one that got away*. He's the one I *sent* away. I didn't feel *good enough* or worthy of him or his wonderful family. Honestly, I saved him a lot of trouble. It's taken me decades to see the truth of it.

I'm so sorry.

After I sabotaged that relationship, I lined up a series of guys who were willing to tell me I wasn't good enough or worthy of love and respect. My self-respect arrived when I was twenty years old. When I finally began to recognize my worth, I met the man who would become my future husband. The first moment I saw him, I turned to my best friend and said, "That's the man I'm going to marry."

We did marry two years later and navigated two decades of highs and lows as a team. Some of the challenges we faced were beautiful, like home renovations and parenthood; others were traumatic, like multiple pregnancy losses, cancer scares, and a near-death experience. Ultimately, we grew apart and in different directions. Couples therapy and a trial separation couldn't bridge the divide. I couldn't see a future without my family, and I wasn't prepared to face the feelings of grief and failure.

When our marriage fell apart, instead of facing those feelings and exploring who I was without a partner, I ignored the wound and, instead, attracted from it. I soaked up external validation from men, which is an unsustainable approach to self-esteem. I ended up falling for a love-bombing narcissist. He charmed his way into my life, and once I was in love, committed and all-in, he became emotionally, financially, and psychologically abusive. I lost almost everything I had worked toward in that relationship, from possessions and home to my identity and sense of self. The impacts of his psychological abuse and discard thrust me into my *dark night of the soul*. It was the most damaging and devastating relationship of my life, and I spent almost a year alone healing physically, mentally, and spiritually.

Looking back, I appreciate the experience because it propelled me through spiritual growth and opened the door to self-love. That self-love is why I left André. I loved him deeply, but I had to love myself equally. Self-love is the *North Star*. The unconditional love of a mother, both my own and my love for my son, are also my guides. I may leave this life with regrets, but love will not be one of them. I do not regret a single relationship. Each one has been a teacher.

As I thought about these relationships and my love for André, I began to feel the weight and grief of it all, and I fell back into sobbing. I cried until my tears ran dry. It grew dark outside, and I missed the dinner hours of the nearby restaurants. I felt empty and hungry. I prayed, *"Am I on the path to my greatest and highest good? Can you give me a sign?"*

At exactly that moment, there was a knock on the door. I opened it to find Alexandra with her ever-present smile standing in front of me with an outstretched plate. On it, there were two freshly baked, small, chocolate cakes, carefully wrapped in bright green banana leaves. *Is it my Birthday?* She said the family was having cake in the dining room and asked if I would like to join them or eat in my room.

"¡Gracias! Comeré en la mesa contigo." (Thank you! I'll eat at the table with you.)

I followed her down the hall and into the dining room, took a seat at the table, and enjoyed warm cake while listening to the boys describe their days at school. I don't know what I did to deserve their kindness and inclusion, but I love the way the Universe wove the thread of their goodness into my story. It was helping me trust that I was on the path; all would be OK; and the next step would be clear when I was ready for it.

I felt a little more at ease, a little more grounded. I felt grateful to this family for creating a protective nest for me while my broken wings healed.

I returned to my room feeling lighter, but I was still unable to sleep. I fell into a continuous stretch around 4 a.m. and awoke to the sound of laughing children playing outside. It was so comforting. Despite my lack of sleep, I felt mentally stronger and ready to face the question: *Should I go to India alone or return home?*

I wasn't sure where I should go, but I felt sure I shouldn't look back. I thought of the story of Lot's wife in the Bible. She looked back and turned to a pillar of salt. The moral of the story is this: Never look back and long for what the Universe is asking you to walk away from. Trust what the Universe has planned for you.

I was ready to talk to those I turn to for wise, grounded counsel. The first was my friend, healer, and spiritual mentor Shmuel. He is the person I trust most in this world to give heart-centered, pure advice. He's a gifted energy healer that a friend referred me to when I was struggling with a broken heart in the aftermath of narcissistic discard. He saved my life. If anyone could speak the truth I needed to hear with gentle grace, it was Shmuel.

February 11
I reached out to Shmuel today.
I told him about the assault, about my situation, and that I am struggling with deciding if I should go to India, or go home and move off the mountain in the middle of winter.

Dearest Tracie,

Sorry to hear about your recent experience. Regardless of the expense, you need to make the trip to India. It is for your own personal healing. If you go back home, you will be in an unsatisfied place, running away. Also, you will carry with you the feeling of what you have missed. See, that trip to India was intended to be just for you. You only. Just as what you gained, created, accomplished in South America was because of what you set out to do there. Keep looking forward with your intention to the new exploration that is solely for you and worthy of you. You are not alone. So far, you have been carrying yourself and others. It is sad that it had this turn of events, but it does not prevent you from continuing this journey. Part of your healing path is to realize how much higher you can climb and grow. You have the company of your inner self. Big hugs, dear sister.

* * *

After reading his words, I remembered something. I had originally booked our trip to India months earlier; however, André was not permitted to apply for a visa because he was Canadian, and at the time, India was not permitting Canadians entry due to a diplomatic row between the two countries. I didn't want to go to India without him, and I especially didn't want to go alone, so we waited until the ban was lifted several months later. I hadn't wanted to travel alone to India, but here I was, *considering* traveling alone to India. The Universe was once again presenting me with the path I wanted to avoid. With Shmuel's perspective, I felt a great unburdening and was more confident in my decision to leave André. I also softened to the idea of traveling alone . . . for my growth.

I sent a text to my mother. I told her I couldn't yet talk about it over the phone (because I knew I'd fall apart), but I wanted to tell her what happened, where I was, and what I was considering. She

37

was supportive, and I felt relief after taking this step. Next I called my best friend Zoya. I needed to tell someone the whole story. I needed to say it out loud. Through tears, I told her everything. She had known me since we were twelve years old, and she'd been there for the highs and lows. She was the least judgmental person I knew with a heart bigger than Texas and boundaries like the Great Wall of China. I could always count on her for heart-centered wisdom. I explained the situation and that my airfare, the biggest portion of the expense, was already purchased and transferable but non-refundable. I confessed I didn't know if I had the strength to do this on my own while heartbroken.

She listened patiently and said, "If there's anyone who can do this, it's you."

Talking to Zoya provided the buoyancy I needed. I let our conversation sink in while listening to the sound of the rain falling outside. I decided to take myself to dinner. I grabbed my raincoat and umbrella and walked toward the lobby where the entire family, Rodrigo, Alexandra, and kids, were sitting together and discussing their day.

Rodrigo perked up and asked, "Where are you going?"

"To dinner," I replied.

He offered an approving nod and smile. Alexandra gave me a wide smile too. They knew this was the first time I had chosen to eat a meal besides breakfast since arriving. I was hungry. I was moving. I was showing signs of life. The little bird was healing.

I returned the smile, "¡Hasta luego!" (See you later!)

I walked a few blocks to Kopal, a charming little restaurant near the edge of a lush pocket of jungle with a hiking trail to a waterfall. The owner had built everything in the place by hand, from the tables and chairs to the wooden menus. It was a romantic spot and candlelit with ambient music. I seated myself at a corner table and felt somewhat awkward sitting there alone. The romantic atmosphere was wasted on the lonely. But was I lonely? I thought

38

about what Wayne Dyer said about loneliness. "You cannot be lonely if you like the person you're alone with." And I did. *I liked me.*

After dinner, as I walked back to the hostel, my thoughts returned to India. Considering how uncomfortable dining alone could feel at times, could I do it? Could I travel the world alone? For most of my life, I had been afraid of being seen. I was a wallflower. I liked being behind the scenes instead of on the stage. I liked spending time alone, but as a woman, I really had to push through *feeling* alone and vulnerable when traveling. I knew plenty of women who didn't feel this at all, but I was not one of them.

Why did I feel afraid? My partners had always provided me with a perceived level of protection or insulation from the outside world. People approached me when I was solo but rarely when I was with a man. Could I face being visible, vulnerable, and alone? Did I want to face it or shrink in the face of it?

I thought of all the times I had traveled alone. What made this trip to India different? The reality was, I wouldn't feel safe with André's presence now.

I was willing to create my own sense of safety. I had traveled solo across the United States quite a few times. *If anyone can do this, it's you.*

I decided to sleep on it.

I slept through most of the night and woke up feeling better than I had since I arrived. I joined my new family for breakfast and thought about how lucky I was to be staying with an Ecuadorian woman who had briefly lived in Italy and knew how to make espresso. It was an aroma and ritual I found so comforting in the morning.

Alexandra and I found plenty to talk about and passed our phones back and forth like schoolgirls passing notes. The time I spent with her was so uplifting. After the table was cleared, I thanked her profusely, and shared my intention, "I am going to get some fresh air today."

I planned to hike to the nearby waterfall, which would be flowing beautifully after the heavy rain that had moved through overnight. I was actually going to do something!

As I was heading out, and passing through the lobby, there was an American woman who was near my age, standing near the gate. We exchanged greetings, and she asked where I was headed. I told her I was walking to the waterfall and she said, "Oh, me too! Would you like company?"

"Of course!"

I soon learned she was a guest from Florida and was staying with a tour guide in the hostel.

As we walked toward the river, she asked, "So, what brings you to Ecuador?"

I explained that this was my second season working on a reforestation project in the valley. Intrigued, she wanted to know more about my background and my inspiration for the project. I told her of my interest in rainforest conservation, protecting primary forests, sustainable growing methods, and architecture.

She asked, "Why are you here in Baeza? Isn't there a hostel closer to the farm?"

I didn't want to tell her my life story, so I told her a half truth, "I'm done for the season, and I'm passing through Baeza on my way to Quito."

We continued down the path, which was becoming steeper, and we were joined by a stray dog that the locals had named Rubio. We began to talk about our age and the challenges that arise from growing older (like feeling our knees on steep inclines).

She said, "I was out to dinner with a group of Canadians last night, and one of the guys, André, asked if I wanted to join him for an all-night music party. I can't imagine doing that. I'm usually in bed by nine."

I nearly choked. I instantly felt the blood leave my face. I was dizzy and sick to my stomach. All this time, I imagined he was hurting like me or maybe contemplating his actions, but he was socializing and going to all-night parties? It was uncharacteristic of him. He rarely wanted to go out. He was in bed by nine most nights.

My eyes filled with tears, and I stopped in the middle of the path to catch my breath and steady myself. Rubio sat down at my feet staring up at me. She asked if I was OK, and I told her, "I take pride in being honest, so I'm not sure why I didn't tell you the whole truth. I'm not here because my season is over. I'm here because my partner broke my heart, and I left him. I'm here until my flight Sunday."

She looked at me with such kindness and said, "Well, thank you for telling me and for trusting me with that. Do you want a hug?"

"Yes, I do actually."

I'm not sure why the Universe put her in my path, but this piece of the puzzle definitely put things in perspective for me. The absence of contact or an apology from André felt great at that moment. I may not have known where I was going, but I knew what I was leaving.

I returned to my room after the hike and wondered why I ever left. I felt renewed pain. It had only been four days, but this was a setback in my grief. It was also a reality I needed to face. I could not look to André to ease my pain. It was mine. I needed to heal this myself and not let this tragic ending write the rest of my life story.

Moments after reaching that resolve, I received a text from him. My heart sank seeing his name on my phone's screen.

I opened the message.

"I changed my profile picture back to what it was. Seems silly to keep it up after you blocked me from your accounts."

His concern wasn't with my well-being. He didn't offer an apology or anything that would contribute to my healing. He was concerned with removing his social media profile photo, which was a picture of the two of us in happier times. What mattered to him was something superficial and inconsequential. And I considered that maybe, just maybe, that profile photo featuring the two of us smiling, was hindering his ability to find a date for all-night music festivals.

I decided to buy myself flowers. I decided to go to India alone.

I spent the rest of the day rearranging my travel plans. I looked at a map of Rishikesh and located the yoga school we were planning to attend together. I searched for schools in Lakshman Jhula across the river on the opposite edge of the city, so if André decided to continue on the trip, it was very unlikely our paths would cross.

I made a list of ten programs based on student reviews and stared at it. I felt pulled to one of the names. *Samadhi Yoga Ashram. Samadhi. Yes.* I sent the school a message and within a few hours, I learned there was one private room left for the month of March. I reserved the spot.

I found solo female traveler groups online and read the experiences and recommendations of other women who had traveled alone through India. I followed their advice and booked a hotel near the Delhi airport with a shuttle to minimize problems. I had everything in order and a plan spread out in front of me on a dozen index cards, each with information like dates, cities, flights, and lodging. I sent a photo to Zoya and my mother and let them know, "This is happening."

I was filled with excitement and dread. The ten legs of flight ahead would be the longest and farthest I had ever traveled alone. Due to some international booking rule no one with my airline could explain to my satisfaction, I was unable to fly directly from Ecuador to London because my trip originated in the United States. I hoped that since I was changing my airfare, I could shave off a couple of days, but I would have to fly from Ecuador back to Seattle for my flight to London.

Because everything had worked out so far, I was grateful, surrendered control, and accepted the timing.

The thing that worried me the most, and it felt silly to admit, was the thought of handling my baggage on my own through countless transitions in and out of airports, taxis, trains, shuttles, hotels, and buses. I felt a bit overwhelmed at the thought of it. It was so nice to travel with someone who could watch your stuff while you used the restroom or who could wait while you tracked down a cart. I'd be managing four months of clothing and gear (for four countries and climates) on my own. I had one extra-large (seriously huge) backpack, one carry-on duffle containing the things I didn't trust with anyone else (journals, camera, lenses), and my laptop bag. None of them had wheels.

I have done harder things. I can do this.

Everything seemed to be coming together with ease. In a single afternoon I changed seats, flights, and found hotels and a residential program. One month earlier, before everything changed, I applied for enrollment in a *pranic* healing school in Rishikesh, but no course was available during the dates of my stay. The very day I was re-planning this trip, I received a message from the school's owner, informing me that he had decided to provide me with private instruction during the days I requested. I asked him what the charge would be for private instruction, and he replied, "The same. I will not charge you more." I could not believe it.

It felt good to move toward something.

February 12

André communicated via text that he intends to continue on the trip to India. I didn't sleep well last night as I struggled with this. I am afraid to spend money right now. Am I to go on this trip and trust

43

what it will open up in my life? I will have to take on whole expenses that were supposed to be shared, and I have to procure a place to live when I return to the States and will have moving expenses. Like a fool, I loaned André a large chunk of money ahead of this trip, and now, I don't have it when I need it most. I feel angry about this. Angry with myself. This over-giving is rooted in my childhood. I need to examine this idea that loving is over-giving. Or, if the person I love is happy, I am happy. It's a mixture of tending to someone else's needs and self-sacrificing or self-abandoning. I learned at a very young age that my needs weren't important. I learned to tend to others to create safety for myself. My best chance for survival was making sure my father was happy. The fastest way to die was to face his wrath. I learned to stuff all my needs down. I was not allowed to be unhappy. I was to be quiet, unexpressed, and polite. And by polite, I mean I was conditioned to not talk back, react, respond, resist, or push back. I was to take it. I learned to create safety for myself by making sure my father was happy. This set me up for a lifetime of abuse. Right now, I am alone in South America excavating my life but starting to have hope for something new. A better, more tranquil way of life. I have more work to do, and I am afraid to do it. I am afraid to travel alone. I am afraid to be seen. Well, those are the thoughts I have. They are not necessarily true. I have traveled alone. I have been seen, and I have overcome this self-speak. I am confident I can manage this trip. I think all I can hope to accomplish today is hydration, self-care, peace, and reaching out for support. I ate a little bit but feel sick to my stomach. My body is buzzing with energy from nerves or excitement or maybe even energy coming in for support. I am so tired. I'm considering something to help me sleep. My eyes feel like raisins, and I look so ashy. My hair seems to have turned gray overnight. But I am pushing through it and in action. I replied to André and told him I intend to continue on the trip and have rescheduled flights, hotels, and found a new school. He hasn't responded.

* * *

Why am I afraid to be seen? Why am I afraid to travel to India alone? I returned to shadow work prompts to examine my self-limiting beliefs. With no hesitation whatsoever, I identified twenty self-limiting beliefs: *Not good enough. Afraid to be seen or be in the spotlight. Fear of judgment. Not qualified. Not able to do it on my own. Not attractive enough. Too different. I don't belong. I'm too sensitive. I'm a failure in relationships. I attract abusive men. I'm afraid of judgment. I am afraid. I am alone. I am weak. I am overwhelmed. I am lost. I am without purpose. I am unlovable. I am not worthy.* These were my secret beliefs. These were the messages from the external world that I had received and believed. Through these exercises, I connected with my earliest interpretations of male anger and power.

When did I first experience an event that feels similar to this experience? What did I do to survive? How did this event inform my ideas around love and power? I knew these answers. I knew my genesis story. I knew what I had always done to survive since that.

Around the age of two, I was playing with a toy in the living room of my family home. It was a pull toy that was a hound dog or beagle, I think, and it made clicking sounds when I rolled it back and forth. I was happy in my play. My mother was not home or was not present. My father was watching TV and yelled, "Shut up!" from his reclining chair. I didn't really understand. I remember observing him but not understanding. So I kept playing, joyfully clicking away. He sprang from the chair, grabbed me by the throat, and strangled me, while screaming, "I TOLD YOU TO SHUT UP!" and that's the last thing I heard as the room faded to black. I don't remember waking up or anything else from that evening, but I do know it was in that moment that I lost my voice. I learned to be quiet, small, silent, invisible, unseen, and unheard. I learned that joy is dangerous. I learned that anger can annihilate. It was this experience with my father's rage, and every subsequent experience, that taught me not to fight back.

My father would often make threats like, "If you cry, it will be worse," or, "If you don't shut up, I'll shut you up." I learned that I was going to be the home for his rage, and my job was to accept that. I understood that if I fought him, resisted, told anyone, cried, or ran, it would be worse. If I wanted to survive, I had to accept the beatings. And his abuse continued until I was estranged from him at age twenty-two.

In contrast, throughout my childhood, I spent nearly every weekend with my grandfather, and he was the very model of a gentleman. He was a safe, supportive, loving man—the kind of man who serves, protects, has emotional intelligence, and respect for women. He loved his mother and wife, was present in my life, and taught me about divine masculinity without knowing what that was at the time. He was my first hero. He was also an actual hero, a World War II Purple Heart recipient.

I was imprinted with these contrasting views of masculinity, and my adult relationships reflected this polarity. When I met my husband, it was my grandfather's example that allowed me to navigate toward a healthy dynamic. For twenty years during that marriage, I knew safety and was able to express my feelings and opinions, and I felt free. But I had not healed the wounding from my father.

When my marriage ended, that unhealed wound contributed to attracting a narcissist. In that relationship, I wasn't empowered. I shrank and became silent and invisible, and I pretended everything was great, but behind closed doors, it was a nightmare. I kept it all inside. Eventually, my joy ceased. I stopped laughing. I stepped into the role of powerless placeholder for male anger and rage, the role my father prepared me for.

In my relationship with André, I vacillated between both experiences. I had a beautiful life with horrible intermissions. I had lightness and darkness. Heaven and hell. I was now being given the opportunity to make something conscious, but what? Was I the cause? Was I a magnet for anger? I realized that even though I had healed from narcissistic abuse, I had not yet healed the deeper wounding of my childhood, which made me the perfect energetic match for a man looking for a place to put his shame, anger, rage, or blame.

February 13
I read this beautiful quote that perfectly describes my feelings at this time: "Grief is the most honest reflection of love. You would not feel so deeply if you did not first have the capacity to love just as deeply, and that is something to embrace in this world. Remember - you will love, and because of that, you will lose at times, but you will be infinitely better for it." - Bianca Sparacino

* * *

Most of my days in the hostel were spent in the same order: coffee and girl talk with Alexandra; then back to my room to reflect and sit with my feelings. I was crying less. My neck was still stiff, and I didn't have much of an appetite, but I was sleeping better despite the constant energy buzzing in my heart and body. Time passed slowly, and I felt ready to leave and start my journey.

I looked at the calendar and realized that it was Valentine's Day. This caused a sinking feeling in my chest. Even though I tried to rationalize that it was just an event to sell flowers and chocolates, I still felt the sadness of being uncoupled and alone. I decided to take myself to dinner.

I walked to Kopal, settled into a dark corner, and ordered. A father was having dinner with his young daughter in the corner opposite me. She was wearing what I assumed was her finest dress with a matching bow in her hair. I loved that he was showing her this. I loved that I was witnessing this man teaching his daughter that she deserved love, attention, and to feel important.

February 14

Love is worth celebrating in this world. My capacity for love is the quality I appreciate most about myself. I love deeply, and in recent years, learned to love myself in a way I had only extended to others.

The thing that I misunderstood about mature love was that it is not external to me. It is not found in another person. It is not something I need to chase or something I cannot have because I am unworthy, undeserving, or not good enough.

We are born with a beating heart engine that has the ability to create an unlimited supply. And if you're open to it, you can receive an unlimited supply too.

When I have experienced the end of a romantic relationship, I have heard, "But you seemed so happy!" or, "You seemed so in love!" And these observations are true. I am happy. I am the source of my love. I make these feelings. When I see photos of myself happy and in love, I think to myself how lucky I am to live with an open heart.

There are risks to living this way but not regrets.

When we love, we are experiencing our capacity to love. And we need more of that in this world. We need more people walking around with open hearts in spite of the violence, heartbreak, betrayals, and suffering.

* * *

I returned to my room, feeling both gratitude and grief, and cried myself to sleep again.

I don't think I can convey how long the span of that week felt. It was like a year in seven days. Aside from morning coffee with Alexandra and brief outings, every minute had been spent alone in my room, sitting with my feelings, examining my past, my choices, my shadow, and the way I show up in the world amid a blur of sobbing, staring, expansion, retraction, fear, hope, acceptance and disbelief, but mostly disbelief.

My life had unraveled like a cheap sweater. I knew I had to focus on anything I could be grateful for, like the coffee I could smell wafting from the kitchen and my Ecuadorian surrogate family waiting at the dining table.

Over breakfast, I told Alexandra and Rodrigo about my journey with yoga and my decision to continue to India alone to deepen my practice. Their excitement and support for my decision was sincere and endearing.

Rodrigo grabbed his belly with both hands and said, "You can come back and teach me!"

I would love to return to them someday so they could see my face with color and my smile restored. Would I ever see the farm again or the hundreds of trees we had planted, the scores of shrubs and flowers? My beloved orchids, hummingbirds, and community? I felt a connection to this place and couldn't imagine never returning.

Rodrigo informed me that I was in for a very special treat for dinner that evening as Alexandra was making empanadas for all of their hostel guests.

After we cleared the morning dishes, Alexandra began preparing for the feast. She toiled away, mixing dough and cooking savory fillings, rolling out perfect circles, and placing the neatly braided pastries on trays around her kitchen. Whatever she was stuffing them with smelled heavenly.

When the time came to start frying, guests arrived, one by one, filling the dining room and kitchen. It was such a great little gathering and cultural exchange. I ate more than I had all winter, and enjoyed conversations with an adventure guide from North Carolina and his partner, one of their clients, a neighbor, and several other guests. I had no idea that so many people were staying in the hostel. I guess most of them were off on adventures by the time I sat down for breakfast with my hosts each day.

Until this empanada extravaganza, I had been the only guest at their table, which underscored the genuine care and concern they seemed to have for my well-being.

After dinner, I helped Alexandra clear the table; then returned to my room to finish the last details of my plans and to survey my finances.

With all the changes, lost deposits, and new expenses that would have been previously shared, I would have $11 left of my budget for the winter. I had enough to reach the finish line, but I didn't have room for anything else, like dinners out, adventures, or shopping. I'd have to be very disciplined in my spending. To be honest, I had no idea how I was going to pull this off and have the money to move and start over.

Feeling a little low, I decided to write myself a letter of support.

February 15
Look at yourself in the mirror. What do you see? Do you see the face of a woman who is vibrant, loved, having her needs met? Do you see a woman who needs softness and care? Do you feel kind toward her when you see her? Do you have compassion for all she has endured? When will you decide to take care of her the way you have taken care of others? Doesn't she deserve to light up? Doesn't she deserve to smile? Does she deserve the stiffness in her neck right now? You are meant to shine. Are you ready for what you deserve? What you deserve is coming, and so is your purpose. It is time to share and shine your light in the world and to do what you came to do. You don't need André to go forward. You only need faith and an open heart. Rest and practice self-love. Be who you are here to be. Do not fear lack of money, employment, or love. If your heart is open, everything you need will flow to you like a river. In your future, there will be a full table and holidays, laughter, right work, the devoted partner you deserve,

miracles, and anything you can imagine for yourself, as long as you remain open.

* * *

It was a big day for me. I was departing on the most adventurous solo trip I had ever taken. Over the next six weeks, my travels would take me from Ecuador's Quijos Valley to the United States to fly to the United Kingdom; then on to India, where I would study yoga for five weeks.

I had learned so much in Ecuador over the season. My Spanish had improved from that of a toddler to a five-year-old. I spent most days with my hands in the soil tending to plants and trees on the farm. I made lasting friendships and met people with so much to teach me about their farming practices and way of life. I was leaving this country, once again (and in most ways), better than I arrived despite having one of the most difficult experiences of my life. I felt reconnected to the magic of the Universe and the goodness of humanity.

I said difficult goodbyes to Rodrigo, Alexandra, and the boys. Rodrigo said, "You are family now," and he gave me a big bear hug. I hugged Alexandra and began to cry. The boys hugged me too.

I was so grateful for this experience of being with them. I was grateful for their care, hospitality, and friendship. They were the reasons there were smiles between the tears and fears. They would forever hold a special place in my life and heart. Their oldest son loaded my bags into the truck that would take me to Quito, and I took my first step toward the unknown.

February 17
For ten days, I sat with my grief and questioned it. I have wanted to understand what happened—André's assault after fourteen months of increased wellness. I thought our love would win. I believed he

would choose wellness and us. It is my *last day in Ecuador, and it also marks ten days that André hasn't accepted responsibility or apologized. I shared a taxi to Quito with another departing hostel guest and took a room in Rincon de la Puembo. I had an incredible meal, was happy with my own company, and wandered around the flower-filled gardens while the sun was setting. Then, I returned to my room and settled into a king-sized bed with crisp cotton sheets after a hot shower. I don't mind having the whole thing to myself.*

* * *

All of my needs were met. I was safe. I was taking the first steps towards a better future.

Empty Seats

The travel from Ecuador to Seattle was brutal. I regretted having luggage without wheels. Reaching U.S. customs in Orlando, I nearly cried when I discovered no carts were available between the baggage claim and the ground transportation terminal. I would have had to carry nearly one hundred pounds of baggage whether someone was with me or not. And in that realization, there was a deeper realization. I had baggage I'd been carrying my whole life that no one else could carry for me. Maybe it was time to jettison that junk.

I made it through customs and had to hoist my backpack off the floor and onto my back. It must have looked like I was reenacting the scene from *Wild* when Cheryl Strayed (played by Reese Witherspoon) puts on her pack for the first time. Only I was much older, and I had to do it while three entertained border agents stood by laughing. Nothing is more motivating than humiliation. It was humbling, but I loaded my four-season wardrobe on my back, slung my laptop bag over my left shoulder, picked up my duffle in my right hand, and began moving toward my next flight. By the end of that long walk, the muscles of my back, neck, and shoulders were burning.

In a few hours, I'd do it all over again.

I made it to Seattle on time and took a shuttle to my hotel where I would catch some sleep before my next flight. Once checked in, I reorganized my bags and pulled out my tablet to charge it and download a couple of movies for the trip overseas. When I turned it on, I discovered André was still signed in and had recently sent a message to his former lover in Seattle. He was reaching out to reconnect with her since he and I "broke up a couple of weeks ago." I was so hurt by this. He wasted no time moving on. I felt angry, but I thanked the Universe for allowing me to see this, just like serendipitously hearing about the all-night music festival from the hiker. I didn't mean to him what he meant to me. I was reminded that there had been no apology or remorse

57

for the assault. I knew I would need to move on without it. This was the dose of medicine I needed to keep walking away—with my chin up—away from what was not for me.

I can buy myself flowers.

The following morning, I boarded my flight to London alone, and I was seated alone. I *felt* alone. I think I only felt this way because I hadn't yet *chosen* my aloneness. It's not how I wanted to take this trip. I tried to adjust my attitude, given all I had learned since leaving. *I would rather be alone.*

The plane was one of those big Airbus numbers with eight seats per row—two seats at each window and four in the middle. The female flight attendants were costumed in red fitted skirt suits that were a cross between futuristic and Mary Poppins. I couldn't quite place the style. There was a bar in the middle of the plane, mood lighting throughout the cabin, fancy stowaway electronics for movies, and plenty of bathrooms. I had a really nice seat on the right exit row aisle with lots of leg room. The seat to my right toward the window was empty, as were the four seats in the center of the craft. Actually, there were a lot of empty seats.

Long after boarding seemed to be complete, a tall, older gentleman entered the cabin and was directed to his seat. He had an air of sophistication. Maybe it was his height and frame, but he appeared both masculine and elegant. He was nicely dressed with a dark woolen overcoat and knit cap, which he stored in the overhead compartment. He looked at the empty seats in the center, looked at me, then returned to the attendant and asked if he could switch seats.

She said, "Of course, there are plenty of empty seats. Take your pick." He began to walk in my direction and sat down across the aisle from me.

He filled the empty seat next to me.

He immediately extended his hand and introduced himself as Morris Clarke. I soon learned he was a Cambridge-educated civil engineer, born and raised in London. His time was divided between Seattle, his family's cottage in London, and leisure time in the south of France. We hit it off straight away.

He informed me he was returning to London to attend the funeral of his lifelong best friend. He choked up and his eyes filled with tears. I knew this feeling. I placed my hand on his arm and said, "I'm so sorry for your loss." He looked me in the eyes and let himself feel his sorrow for a moment, returning a shy smile.

He has an empty seat beside him too.

He reminded me of my grandfather in every way—his charm, mannerisms, laugh, the same twinkle in his eye, the gift for storytelling, and nostalgia for his close friends. His presence was comforting, like home.

When we were ready for takeoff, our flight attendant, a cheerful and bubbly midlife English woman, took the jump seat facing us in the exit row and joined us in conversation. She explained she had just started this daily route between London and Seattle, so Morris and I shared tips for visiting the city and other nearby areas. When I informed them this was my first time visiting London, they were excited for me to explore *their* city and peppered me with questions. *Where are you staying? Where are you going? What are you doing? You're going alone?!* They shared tips and pointers on neighborhoods to visit, areas to avoid, and the best theaters.

Once we were in the air, our favorite attendant excused herself and set about her duties. Soon after, the first beverage service arrived, and a young flight attendant asked Morris what he would like to drink. He answered, "Champagne in a proper glass."

The attendant said, "Oh, I'm afraid that's not possible, but you could try the cash bar in First Class."

He looked at me and asked, "What should I order?"

I shrugged and he ordered a rum. Then he turned back to me with a sparkle in his eye and grinned, "It doesn't hurt to ask." He then proceeded to tell me several stories about times in his life when he asked for what he wanted. The first was when a developer in Boston wanted him to manage a huge construction project. He told the developer he didn't like Boston but would take the job if the company would pay for his room and board at the Ritz Carlton in New York City and allow him to commute from there. To his surprise, he was offered not only what he asked for but was allowed to expense concierge services and theater tickets to the company.

His next story was just as surprising. He confessed his love of opera and said many years earlier, he was traveling through Venice with a lady friend and timed his arrival on Thursday evening specifically, so he could attend dress rehearsal at the Venice Opera House. Arriving there, they inquired when rehearsal would begin, and the house manager said, "I'm sorry, sir; we had our dress rehearsal last night."

Morris described being mystified by this and responded, "But Thursday is the customary night of the dress rehearsal worldwide!"

The house manager purportedly excused himself while they explored the opera house but returned moments later to report the performers, stage hands, and musicians were coming in for a special dress rehearsal just for them. Morris and his lady friend were seated in the "Royals Box" and enjoyed a romantic private performance. As I listened to him talk, I realized how different my life might have been if I had asked for what I wanted or needed.

After our first meal, Morris began his third story. Many years ago, after a long day of travel, he hadn't eaten very much, so when he returned to London famished, he went straight to his favorite restaurant but found it was closed. He knocked on the door, and the maître d' answered. Morris asked if he would open for him so he could get a steak.

The maître d' said, "I'm afraid that's not possible. The chef has a special guest. The house is closed."

The chef, hearing voices in the dining room, popped his head out from the kitchen and said, "Let Morris in. I will cook for him." When he entered the kitchen, the special guest was Diana Spencer who would later become Princess Diana.

"I swear this is true," he said.

Moments later, our conversation was interrupted by our favorite cheerful flight attendant who leaned in and discretely said, "I heard you would like some bubbly. I've got you covered." She gave us a wink and walked away only to return moments later with a tray. On it were two glasses of champagne, *in proper glasses*, two fine chocolate bars, and an assortment of snacks just for us. I couldn't believe it. I'd never gotten anything but ginger ale in a plastic cup in Saver Fare class, and here I was getting treated like a queen while getting a free master class in manifestation.

Morris and I toasted our new friendship and spent the next four-and-a-half hours laughing until my cheeks were seizing in protest. I helped him open condiment packages that were too difficult although, I suspect he could do it and simply enjoyed me fussing over him. In exchange, he entertained me and made me feel like I was a little girl again, sitting at my grandfather's side and listening to stories of adventure.

Around 2:30 in the morning, we agreed we should try to sleep a bit. We both settled into our reclined chairs and slept until morning coffee service. And then, our conversation started right back up again. He told me of his life as an engineer, pilot, motorcycle racing team manager, and heli-skier (according to him, he was one of the most experienced in the world). He spoke of his family's engineering legacy in England; they built the toll roads for Henry VIII and had been building ever since; his exotic travels; and his love of ballet and opera.

Morris described seeing the Rolling Stones play a gig in the Chislehurst Caves before they were an international sensation and the remarkable woman that became his friend, Princess Diana. He was the world's most fascinating man, and I was surprised I had never heard of him before our paths crossed. He needed to teach people to live or lie—I wasn't sure which. His stories were so incredible I could hardly believe him. But I had just witnessed him get exactly what he asked for without being rude, pushy, or entitled. When he heard no, he didn't resist or push back, and he didn't lose his smile. He smiled like he knew it would come to him anyway. And maybe I had this magic in me too. After all, I suddenly had the best company I could ask for.

I was so grateful to the Universe for the gift of Morris Clarke. It turned out, I wasn't lonely during my flight overseas. The empty seat was filled. And you know what? If I had flown directly from Ecuador to London, I would have missed out on that experience.

Trust the timing.

Like a seer, Morris said, "You have to go to Monte Carlo." He looked me directly in the eyes when he said this and squinted a little as if he were an actual fortune teller reading my mind and envisioning my future. Then he nodded in self-confirmation and said, "Yes. Yes. You must go to Monte Carlo. You will love it. I know you will love it."

He told me he once worked on a project at Saint Paul's Cathedral in London, and there was a staircase that went all the way to the top of the highest dome. "You simply must visit the cathedral, find the staircase, and go to the top. Yes, promise me you'll go to the top. You can see the entire city from there. Promise."

I promised him I would do it. We exchanged numbers and agreed to stay in touch.

We disembarked around 9:30 a.m. I collected my baggage and made my way via taxi to my hostel in Hyde Park. It felt strange to sit alone in the back seat of the taxi. I'm not sure why. There was an empty seat beside the driver and an empty seat beside me. There was an unspoken rule, I guess.

The trip from Heathrow to Hyde Park offered my first view of England, and I marveled at the gardens and architecture. It was bustling and affluent with a surprising amount of greenspace.

I arrived at my hostel, one of dozens of identical structures with black, iron coach lamps and fences lining the street. I checked in with the office and was informed that my room was a block away, around the corner, so I *not-so-joyously* lugged my baggage on my aching frame a little further to my private room, which was the size of a broom closet. My room in Ecuador was huge and $20 per night. This room was tiny and six times the price, but I had everything I needed. There was a twin bed, a small desk (more like a wall shelf), and the tiniest bathroom I'd ever seen with more lights than square footage.

I caught my reflection in the mirror and saw the huge shocks of gray and white in my hair that weren't present two weeks earlier. In a few days, my face appeared to have aged years. I'd heard of this happening during stressful events, but I was not ready for this phase! I had this realization that I could potentially re-enter the dating scene in my fifties, and the thought of that made me feel a certain level of dread and panic that I wasn't expecting. I don't consider myself vain, but I immediately walked straight to the nearest drugstore and bought hair color, anti-aging cream, hydrating potions, and petroleum jelly because my friend Lily swears that's the secret sauce when you look like a bog witch. I had an impromptu spa day in my tiny room and spent the evening planning the week ahead.

As I reviewed my travel guide, notes, and plans, I discovered the two plane tickets I bought to Venice months earlier and realized I never canceled the flights or the pre-paid room. It was supposed to be a little romantic side trip to the place André spent the summers of his youth, just a two-hour flight from London. He was planning to show me his aunt's house, the places he played, and his favorite swimming spot. It's purportedly the most romantic city in the world and home to some of the most beautiful architecture in Europe. I thought of Morris Clarke's story of the Venice Opera house and stared at the departure time and what it would mean for me. If I went, I'd have to navigate the train system in London and the ferry in Italy.

I decided to keep the trip because I'd always wanted to see the city; the sea levels were rising; and because I could. I knew keeping this side trip would likely impact my budget since Venice is an expensive city, but I would lose the non-refundable airfare and room if I didn't go.

Day one, and I was already starting to fret about the financial realities of each decision.

Fuck it. I'm taking myself to Italy!

I had a hard time falling asleep but managed a solid run of a few hours before waking to the sound of steady rain. I had never been so tired and dehydrated in my life. I couldn't even tell you how many time zones I'd been through in the five days prior . . . South America, across U.S. Eastern, Central, Mountain, Pacific; then back again and across the Atlantic Ocean to the United Kingdom.

I ventured out and purchased an umbrella with what remained of my $11 budget surplus; Then I popped into a little Italian cafe called *Mimo's* near Paddington Station.

The place was operated by a multi-generation family, and as I approached the counter, each of them greeted me. The all-male ensemble elbowed each other, pretending to fight over who would get to take my order and who would get to make my coffee. Once my latte was ready, they pretended to fight over who got to hand it to me, and the youngest said, "Come back tomorrow! I will make your coffee!" and the eldest retorted, "If he makes it, you'll never drink coffee again!"

When the barista handed me my cup, he winked and gestured towards the other, "I hope I don't make him mad."

Not only did they serve fine Italian espresso, but I would return every day just for the fuss they made over me. Their harmless flirtations lifted my spirits and were like an elixir for the new gray in my hair and the post-midlife dating fears that had surfaced.

I took my coffee and umbrella and started my exploration. I sent Zoya an update and told her about the charming Italians, and moments later, she wired me $50 and told me to buy my coffee there every day. I loved that my friend wanted that for me. I was so grateful to have her in my life.

How lucky am I?

I walked eight miles along the canal and wandered in and out of gardens with wrought iron gates and through Paddington, Hyde Park, Marble Arch, and Knightsbridge; then to Buckingham Palace and back, all in the rain. I started to remember who I was. I loved exploring cities with maps. I love art and architecture. I love traveling. For the first time, I felt proud of myself for leaving André. I was proud that I chose to prioritize my own safety and well-being.

I returned to my broom closet, completed the online check-in for my flight to Venice, and packed my overnight bag.

February 23

I slept nine hours and woke up refreshed and excited for the first time in over two weeks. I went to see my favorite Italians for a large esteem latte, then walked along the canal and through the park before returning to my room to pack my bag for Venice.

I walked two miles to Victoria Station and successfully navigated the rail but only because of the endearing quality Londoners have to over-explain everything. At first, I thought it was just my house manager's way. When I checked in at the front desk of the hostel, she made a map of the square city block for me and demonstrated with arrows how to walk around the block either way to find the best

Indian restaurant in the area. I'm not saying I would take one look at me, an American, and assume I can navigate a square without getting lost, but she gave me a presentation with pauses every two sentences, "Yeah? You follow?"

I heard the best over-explanation yet while waiting for my train. The announcer's voice came over the speaker to share, "We regret to inform you that the train to (inaudible) is delayed because a bunch of construction workers made a mess with rubbish on the tracks, and they have yet to clean up their handiwork. We're so deeply sorry. And also, don't forget to watch your belongings carefully at (inaudible) because there is an unfortunate number of unsavory characters and thieves in that area. It's dreadful, really."

* * *

My train was on time, mostly empty, and had free Wi-Fi, so I caught up on messages and planned my must-see list for the *City of Love*.

My flight was easy and comfortable. It was late evening and dark when I arrived at the Marco Polo airport, and when I passed through customs, I requested that my passport be stamped after it was scanned. That stamp felt like a merit badge.

I made my way to the water taxi stand, purchased my ticket, and waited to board my boat with two dozen tourists and their luggage. There was a line of docks with sleek and sexy, mahogany, mid-century boats, and I immediately recalled childhood weekends spent in my grandparents' beautiful Chris-Craft on Buckeye Lake in Ohio. My grandmother always looked like a movie star in the front seat with oversized sunglasses and her hair tied in a scarf. Those were core memories for me. The smell of the water, the sun dancing on the lake, wind in my hair without a care, and sparkling mist in our wake. That era seemed to be preserved here where

66

glossy wooden boats bobbed up and down in the dark water of night while moonlight dazzled on its surface.

Ours was a long boat referred to as the "water bus" that accommodated about thirty. It was decidedly unsexy. We all boarded and went below deck where bench seating lined the cabin under a row of windows on both sides. It was dark, so there was nothing to see during the trip from the mainland to the island of Venice, which took about an hour. I could see the lights as we approached, and the boat slowed to a crawl as it began to glide through the Grand Canal. Everyone pressed their nose to the glass to see the beauty of the water reflecting lights from the shops and bridges along this main route through the city. The marble Rialto Bridge spanned the channel and was a sight to behold. When we passed under it, something magical stirred in me—a combination of butterflies, awe, and disbelief. *Am I really here?*

The water taxi came to a stop. I disembarked and pulled out the handwritten directions to my accommodations. I was not prepared for how spooky the place felt at night. It was a little unnerving to navigate alone in the dark. Once you stepped away from the main canal, lights were few and far between, and because of the height of the buildings, the only way the moon could illuminate the passageways was if it were directly overhead. There weren't streets, but there were corridors between towering, old four-and-five-story structures. The buildings were hundreds of years old, and I noticed every beautiful wood and iron-hinged door I passed.

I found my first mark, turned left, and began navigating but got a bit turned around and had to go back the way I came and start over again. This time, I got it right and ended up in the Campo Manin, a large courtyard in front of my host's building. Finding the entry door was the next challenge. I walked around the perimeter three times before realizing the numbers were not in order. I found the door and rang the intercom.

The owner answered the call button and unlocked the door, and I entered to find an empty reception area with a laptop sitting on a desk. On the laptop screen, a remote agent appeared on video to check me into my suite and tell me where to locate my key. This technology was an interesting contrast to the five-hundred-year-old doors and fourteen-foot ceilings.

I climbed the red carpeted stairs and went down the long hallway adorned with gilded mirrors to find my room. I turned the skeleton key, opened the door, and began to fall in love. The room was as big as a house. It had a huge bed with a velvet tufted headboard and a gilt wood frame. There were Venetian chandeliers, gorgeous hand-knotted carpets, inward opening windows bedecked with heavy floor-to-ceiling velvet drapes over sheers, and massive wood shutters that opened out to the courtyard. I felt like a queen. Except, for a queen, this would be her everyday environment, so she probably wouldn't feel the way I did at that moment. I felt like a giddy child.

I jumped on the bed. I fainted onto the couch. I touched every glass on the bar. I opened the shutters and windows and waved at no one. The bathroom was luxurious, and larger than my entire hostel room in London. I savored every detail and took the longest shower I had taken in years, which was highly irresponsible, I know. I still felt an ache in my neck, but I was healing.

I'm going to heal it. All of it.

When I finally climbed into bed for the night, I curled up along the side, as I usually do, but I could feel the space and emptiness of the bed. So, I stretched out wide like a starfish and claimed all of it. No one was missing.

I expected to be awakened by several ghosts and the sounds of haunting things, but I slept great and woke up excited to open those big windows and see Venezia in the daylight. I drew the curtains back, opened the windows, and turned the shutters out to find gondolas gliding on the water below and scores of people crossing the square at various angles. I made coffee and sat at the bistro table by the window; propped my heels on the empty chair, and took it all in. What must it have been like to see this place centuries before? Oh, the wonder of it all!

The sun was shining, so I ventured out to get lost in the city. Without a plan.

From the moment I stepped onto the street, I was smiling from ear to ear. Seeing this place in the light of day left me in awe. The architecture was influenced by Gothic, Renaissance, and Byzantine styles. There were beautiful ornaments and details everywhere, like figural, iron door hardware, glass window panes placed in the age of Caravaggio, marble bridges, cobblestone streets, and sculptures.

As I made my way to the Basilica di San Marco, I paused to photograph art, people, and every fine detail. When I reached and entered the plaza, I was overwhelmed with emotion. My eyes filled with tears, and my heart swelled at the sight of the cathedral. I don't have the words to describe the magnitude or beauty. I roamed the grounds soaking up every detail; then I was hungry and decided to eat small bites in out-of-the-way cafes to keep my expenses down.

I made my way across the bridge to San Paulo on the opposite side of the Grand Canal, where I found a little sidewalk cafe with a beautiful view. No one was sitting outside, so I entered the establishment and came face-to-face with, well—nearly ran into—a handsome brown-eyed man with long, black hair, neatly tied at the back of his neck. His crisp, white shirt perfectly contrasted the tan of his skin.

Startled, I said, "Oh, I'm sorry. Excuse me."

He just smiled widely and stared into my eyes as if he'd been waiting for me to arrive.

"I would like to sit outside. Is this possible?"

"Of course," he said shyly, without breaking eye contact.

I had my choice of outdoor tables, so I chose the one nearest the water's edge. The waiter I nearly ran over in the entry brought me a menu, and once again, his eyes locked with mine.

He said, "I'm sorry. I hope it is okay to say—your eyes are beautiful."

I felt a tinge of self-awareness, but I often get compliments on my blue-gray eyes in areas where most people are brown-eyed. Less than 1 percent of the population had my eye color, so I didn't think too much of it. I thanked him. He poured a glass of water and placed a menu on the table, but instead of walking away to give me time with it, he asked, "Why is a beautiful woman like you alone in a place like this?"

Did he just call me beautiful?

I laughed, "That's a good question."

He said, "I will show you this city. I work until nine, but we will meet at the bridge, and I will show you all the beautiful places."

I felt my cheeks blush. I was pretty sure this man was fifteen years younger than me, but he was serious. I said, "Thank you, but I'm leaving soon and I can't."

He asked, "What is your name?"

"Tracie."

"Tracie is a name as beautiful as you."

I thanked him and said, "I'm very flattered, and I am quite a bit older than you."

He looked puzzled, "How old are you?"

"Fifty-three."

He scoffed, "This is nothing. This is no problem. I work until nine. Then we will meet at the bridge."

"No, I can't. I have a flight to catch in the middle of the night."

"Where are you going?" he asked.

"Well, back to London; then on to India."

70

"Tracie, you are here now. You are single. I am here now. I am single. We may never have this chance again. I just know you are not getting on that plane. You'll see. Someday, you will be here, and we will be married, looking at all this together," he said as he gestured to the water and city. "Say *yes*. Meet me at nine."

A part of me almost said yes because he was selling me on the dream—the *living in Venice* dream. The *not getting on the plane* dream. Would it be so bad to marry for companionship and citizenship, so I could spend the rest of my life writing in cafes, getting fat on *cannolis,* and drinking fine espresso? But instead, I said, "I'm flattered, but I can't."

He smiled a beautiful smile and said, "Hand me your phone. I'll give you my number."

I obliged, and he sent himself a message from my phone: "My name is Gio. Now you have my number, so when you change your mind, you can tell me you're meeting me at the bridge."

While he held my phone, I noticed his features and hands, and wondered if I could ever fall out of love with André. I missed his hands, hugs, and forehead kisses. The reality was the André I loved only existed in my memories now.

I broke from my daydream and realized Gio was still staring at me, but not in a creepy way. It was more like the way you look at someone you haven't seen in a long time and you just forgot their face and what it felt like to be in their company.

I shook my head, as if I had just woken up, and joked, "Wait a minute, did you just propose to me?"

He laughed and said, "Don't worry, there's time. You'll see. Meet me at the bridge at nine."

I ordered coffee and a cannoli and as soon as he delivered them, a pigeon landed on the empty chair beside me. I broke off a piece of pastry and placed it on the edge of the table. The bird stared at me too.

See, life will go on.

Other patrons had filled the once empty tables around me, and they were craning their necks to see around Gio to, perhaps, witness love in bloom. Two older Italian men, who were seated to my right, appeared to be rooting for my new suitor.

I wondered what would happen if I showed up at that bridge at nine. Something nefarious? Something innocent? I held out another piece of cannoli, and the bird took it from my hand. Gio returned to the table and said loudly, with both arms stretched wide as if performing for the other guests now, "See! *Even birds love you Tracie*!" Then, with one finger pointing in the air in victorious proclamation, he said, "Tonight at nine!"

He walked away backwards and the pair of Italians leaned their heads forward with raised eyebrows, ready to cheer for my "*Yes*!" I smiled at them and shook my head. In unison, their shoulders sank, and they shrugged in disappointment while the pigeon and I finished our dessert.

I settled my tab and left quickly while Gio was busy with the growing crowd. As I continued on, wandering through the city, I dismissed the experience as something akin to a Venetian performance. I figured single men seduced lonely female tourists in the *City of Love,* so that both could touch romance and be less lonely for a little while. But, if I'm really honest, the deeper thought was, *I am unworthy.*

For the rest of the day, I covered most of the city, walking into any building that was open to the public. I found the Venice Opera House and stood inside admiring it, imagining Morris Clarke running up the steps, pulling his lady friend along, eager to get to the rehearsal that wasn't. Funny to be standing here in his footsteps after just meeting him days ago. *Morris Clarke would probably go to the bridge at nine.*

Venice was a sensual experience. Aside from the visual beauty in every detail, so many smells mingled in the air—cologne, bread, coffee, and fresh flowers, but they all worked together to create an olfactory experience with water as a base note. Music was ever present, wafting through the air from cafes and restaurants. The Italian language is the most beautiful to the ear. Then, there's the food. Oh, the decadent food. Venice is living proof of what can be made manifest when the heart inspires creation instead of the mind.

Later in the afternoon, while I sat in a plaza drinking tea and watching a man untangle the leashes of the six dogs he attempted to walk at once, I received a message from Gio:

> *In life, a person does not get chances every day, and if they get chances, they should take them. Remember me... at 9 o'clock, we will eat tiramisu on the bridge.*

His tenacity brought a smile to my face. *Did he really just up the ante with dessert? Tiramisu is my kryptonite.* I was resolved and did not reply, but he opened my eyes to something I hadn't experienced in a long time. *Sweetness.* The sweetness of being admired. The sweetness of being seen. The sweetness of feeling beautiful.

I walked a bit lighter for the rest of the day, pausing on bridges several times to watch lovers cuddled in gondolas while gondoliers sang songs that reverberated between centuries-old structures. I took pictures for couples, young and old, and their love warmed my heart. I decided I could live in Venice, with all of its architecture, lovers, theaters, cafes, restaurants, museums, artists, craftsmen, and people watching, *if* there were more green space. That was the only missing piece for me.

I was starting to get used to the *table for one* while also appreciating that I could stop to look at anything I wanted to admire. I was on *my* schedule. I studied every leaded glass window, door knocker, and iron latch. This love of detail was something my past partners tolerated but didn't understand. Between random pangs of sadness and wishing, I was also in love in the *City of Love*, but I recognized another feeling I wanted more of. Freedom. I felt free to be myself.

I spent the rest of the night wandering, lost in the twisting, turning corridors, and squares. Lost but finding my way.

I exhausted myself seeing it all and returned to my room around 8:45 p.m. Fifteen minutes later, my phone rang, and I stared at it.

Don't answer it.

It stopped ringing, and I felt relief. At 9:16, I received a text message. A simple "???" from Gio, and I didn't reply to that either.

My water taxi was scheduled to depart at 3:48 a.m., so once again, I had to navigate the winding corridors in the dark. It was very easy to get lost in the narrow passages, and it felt spooky to wander through the city while everyone was asleep. I made several wrong turns into dead ends and started to feel panic. If I missed the waterbus, I would miss my flight, and I had no room in my budget for mistakes. Thankfully, I arrived at the dock with only a few minutes to spare.

Aboard the boat I watched the lights of Venice fade to dim, and when the boat was a safe distance from Venice, I sent Gio a message.

Thank you for your kindness. I am on my way to India. I know you will meet your girl soon . . . the one who will meet you on the bridge.

I recently went through a painful heartbreak, and you really lifted my spirits at a time I needed it. Thank you.

He replied quickly, and I was surprised that he was awake at that early hour:

"I'm so sorry to hear that someone broke your heart. It shouldn't have happened because you have a very good heart. I felt your loneliness so I asked to meet you. I also live alone here. But you did not accept my offer to meet, and I think we were meant to. It's really

sad for us. I was sure that if we both met, we would both be very happy, and we would have this moment to remember."

Gio, I will remember the moment ~ Tracie

Within five hours, I was back in London. I took the train from Gatwick to Victoria Station and then had a two-mile walk to my hostel. I returned to my broom closet and fell into bed. For the entire return trip, my mind was filled with fond memories of André. *Is there life beyond this? Could anyone ever love me the way I love?* I felt sadness creep in again. There was an ebb and flow to this feeling. Somedays, I was awash with it, and others, the feeling dissolved, and I felt my strength.

After a brief rest, I went to see the Italians, and they made their usual fuss over me. I ordered tea so one of them asked, "No coffee? Is everything okay?" I nodded. The eldest brother walked around the counter, looked me in the eyes, and asked, "You drink it here?"

I said, "No, to go please."

He placed his hand gently behind my elbow and said, "No, please, you drink it here." And he pointed to his brother.

While handing me my tea in a china cup, the brother said, "See! I got to hand it to you!"

The eldest then said, "Let me." And with his hand again gently behind my elbow, barely touching, he walked me to a table for two, pulled out the chair, and gestured for me to sit. He placed one hand on my shoulder ever so lightly and gave it two gentle pats, as if to say *stay.*

I swear I think those guys knew what I was going through. They lifted my spirits each time I walked through their door. I sat in the middle of their cafe alone, and my eyes began to water even though I was surrounded by cheerful chatter. Men were talking about fights and fighters, hilariously but lovingly harassing each other over their neighborhood of origin or football team loyalty.

And for that moment, I let myself belong there, and I drank my tea slowly from a proper china cup with a warm, grateful heart.

People keep showing up in ways that surprise me.

I thanked my favorite Italians for the tea and left them better than they found me. I spent the afternoon exploring Hyde Park and Kensington Gardens and decided to have a traditional English experience, so I popped into the pub on my block and grabbed a high table just as the after-work crowd started to pour in. I ordered fish and chips and a ginger beer, which garnered hilarious needling from the local ale drinkers, who had no idea the pub served non-alcoholic beverages. Then, I enjoyed watching my first ever game of cricket on the telly.

One of the things that I noticed in London establishments was that people seemed to interact with regard. Well, what I perceived as regard. Even the flirting I encountered was respectful. (To be fair, it was the Italians doing the flirting.)

On the street and in public spaces, people didn't make eye contact. I had walked twenty miles and passed probably thousands of people, but very few returned my gaze or greeting. Man, I tried. I said hellos, smiled, and attempted to connect.

This was in stark contrast to South America where everyone greets you when you pass. If I was walking down the sidewalk in Ecuador and passed three people, I would hear three, *"Buenas noches."*

February 26
At three o'clock in the morning, I was startled awake by my ringing phone. I answered, and it was my ex-husband, John.
He said, "Hey, I wanted to let you know, I just sold the house, and I made a nice profit on it. I want to send a little bit of money your way since you contributed so much to increasing its value."

I could hardly believe my ears. John and I had been divorced for almost twelve years. He continued to live in the house we owned together, while I moved into a nearby townhouse.

It's true, I put a lot of love into the house and gardens, but what brought this on? Was the Universe working through him? I felt completely stunned.

We talked for a couple of hours, and somehow, we got on the subject of forgiveness. We agreed we wanted it expressed, not just assumed. We were best friends for twenty-two years, and I was so glad we still had that friendship. It was such a healing conversation, and it made me feel like less of a failure in relationships and, in general.

* * *

I awoke to an alert of an electronic funds transfer into my bank account. Without having any idea what my financial situation was, John had deposited enough money to cover what I lost rescheduling flights, booking hotels, and changing schools, plus enough to help with my move when I returned home. I began to cry tears of joy. I had taken this leap and the Universe came through for me. Here was this remarkable and timely gift that appeared unexpectedly and without asking anyone but the heavens. I hadn't told one single person about my financial situation. I didn't have to fret over my decision any longer. The entire Universe seemed to be conspiring through others to move me forward.

Things like this don't happen to me. The people showing up, the kindness, the generosity, the care, the help.

I was so humbled. I called John and thanked him profusely, and then I told him the truth about why I was traveling alone. I felt ashamed to admit it to him. In our twenty-two-year relationship, I can't think of a single time he called me a name or raised his voice. I shared with him my commitment to healing my deepest wound on this journey—the wounding caused by my father.

I am going to return home, wherever that is, with less baggage.

With new resolve, I went to see the Italians for my daily cup of esteem, and then went straight to the bus stop and set out to find St Paul's. I promised Morris Clarke that I would go to the cathedral, find the staircase, and climb it to the top of the dome, so I could see the view of London from above.

When I heard the bus driver announce my stop, I made my way to the door, waited for it to fold open, and stepped off the double-decker to find the cathedral looming large over the street; its west clock tower was overpowered by its massive dome. I wandered into the foyer of this magnificent structure, which had been constructed in 1710 by the church that was founded on the site in AD 604. Then I opted for the self-guided tour.

There were at once a dozen groups led by docents and religious services being observed in the rotunda. There was so much to see within these walls and, to be honest, it felt more like a war memorial than a devotional space. There were impressive sculptures depicting heroes of battle and memorial plaques for the fallen. There was even a beautiful chapel dedicated to Americans, who had sacrificed their lives protecting England during World War II.

One could make a lifetime study of the beautiful stone floors, arches, and the incredible detail found in the woodwork.

In college, I studied, researched, and wrote papers on many of the places I had seen throughout Venice and London, including St Paul's Cathedral. My Art History professor, Matt Auvinen, a marble sculptor, was passionate about his subject, and that passion was infectious. As a student, I lived vicariously through his teachings and descriptions, but couldn't fully appreciate his enthusiasm until I stood in the grand scale of these places and wondered at the skill and labor necessary to bring each of them to life. No photograph, description, or film can replace *experiencing*. The human interest in art, craftsmanship and aesthetics, were on display here. They seemed to peak before the Industrial Revolution. Or rather, maybe the Industrial Revolution dulled our sense of magic and pride in our work. Maybe we don't dream big anymore.

I found the stairs to the dome and started my climb. First, I was ascending a broad, enclosed spiral staircase. It was wide enough that four people could stand shoulder to shoulder on each step at once. The higher I climbed, the more the stairs narrowed, until finally I was climbing an open iron staircase wide enough for one, suspended in what felt like a tower. The temperature dropped considerably in this space, and I could hear the howl of the wind outside. I could see through the risers under my feet and judge the distance to the floor below, so I had to stop looking down. I could feel movement in the frame and wondered if these stairs had been inspected in the past three centuries.

What have I promised?

I began to feel a little scared. I'd never been afraid of heights, but that was changing.

I had started counting steps from the main floor of the cathedral, and when I reached the top, I had climbed 528 stairs. I opened the door against the force of the blowing wind just as the tower clock below was about to strike eleven, and I was there for every toll. I kept my word. I was once again standing in Morris Clarke's footsteps. I was not the first to be there, nor the bravest, but I was there.

As I leaned cautiously against the railing, feeling unnerved by the wind and the height, I understood why Morris made me promise to take in the spectacular, 360° view of London from this perch. It was like looking down from the heavens on a perfect little scale model.

I thought of Morris wandering through the town below at every phase of his life. I imagined him as a teen, making mischief with his band of brothers; then as a college student whisking girls away on motorbike adventures to see bands in caves along the shore; then as a restless but disciplined engineer, and finally, an accomplished man of the world. I thought of all the events and experiences that had to take place from the time Morris was born until the day our paths magically intersected at precisely the moment I needed to hear his life story.

I was grateful to this city for its part in shaping such an interesting fellow. The world needs more people like Morris Clarke —people who remind us to live fearlessly, to ask for what we want, and to keep the sparkle in our eyes when we hear "no," or when we are rejected because what is meant for us will always arrive.

I went back down all 528 stairs and explored the crypt under the cathedral floor where there were many tombs and memorials, such as that of Florence Nightingale. Like most magnificent things created in this world, this foundation rested on the dead. And maybe that was what I was meant to consider. I was starting over on the ash and bones of my former life.

I continued my adventure and visited London Bridge, the Tower of London, Westminster Abbey, Westminster Cathedral, and finally the Natural History Museum. I logged about ten miles on foot, and the crisp air was clearing and invigorating. For the longer stretches, I hopped back on the bus. The warmth, the hum of the motor, and the gentle sway during these rides was relaxing, and my mind would wander to thoughts of André and the life I had planned—the life that disappeared in an instant. Just weeks before, I was in Ecuador, grieving, wondering if I could make this trip alone but the Universe supported me every step of the way.

When I left André, I was hurting, afraid, and had no idea what would happen next, and the Universe gave me a safe place to heal and the love of a family. I felt nervous about traveling alone but set out on the adventure anyway, and the Universe sent me Morris Clarke. I was concerned about money but took a huge leap of faith, and money showed up miraculously.

My confidence was returning with each little victory, like navigating the corridors in Venice or London's rail system. My heart was softening with each new connection and smile. I was feeling like I could start over and build a stronger version of me. On the ashes and bones.

I felt grateful and held by love. At that moment, all of the seats were filled.

Living with Ghosts

There was internet service on my flight to India, so about an hour prior to landing in New Delhi, I used my hotel's messaging service to schedule my shuttle pickup at the airport.

The customer service agent answered promptly, "I'm sorry; we don't have a shuttle. You will need to use the pre-paid taxi stand in the ground transportation area."

I started to feel dread. I had specifically chosen this hotel because it listed "airport shuttle" as an amenity, and I wanted to avoid getting in a cab from the airport in New Delhi after reading dozens of cautionary tales from travelers. I didn't want my fear to manifest a poor outcome, so I decided not to worry and to trust that it would work out OK.

I realized I needed to switch the eSIM in my phone from the United Kingdom to India, but just as I was making the change, the pilot announced internet service would cease for the remainder of the flight, and electronic devices should be stowed in preparation for landing.

The eSIM is a modern wonder that allows travelers with smartphones to switch to local networks in most countries. The snag with the eSIM I used was that I could only switch between countries and update the carrier when internet service was available, and I had just lost my internet service, so I'd have to take care of the switch once I was able to join the airport's public Wi-Fi. I made a mental note to take care of that while I was waiting at the baggage carousel for my luggage. I also wanted to find one of the two bank machines I had located on the terminal map, so I could withdraw Rupees.

It was an uneventful flight and landing, and I'm always quite grateful for those. I made my way through customs, presented my papers, and my passport was stamped, which felt like a finish line and starting line at the same time.

I had arrived in India.

While I was at the baggage claim, I once again tried to switch my eSIM, but there was no available public Wi-Fi in the airport at that moment. I found both bank machines, but each was out of service, I presumed because the internet was unavailable. I started to feel concerned and recognized my planning wasn't quite working out the way I had hoped. I had no airport shuttle; I was not able to use my mobile phone, and I had no currency in a country that preferred cash over cards.

I went to the currency exchange counter and gave them all twenty U.S. dollars I had in my pockets in exchange for Rupees. I figured I should be OK without cash for a short period because my accommodation was prepaid, and I was only going to the hotel to sleep for a few hours before my next departing flight to Dehradun. I hoped I would find an ATM in the departure area the following morning, but if not, there was another bank machine at the next airport.

I made my way to the taxi stand and prayed they would accept a credit card. The counter attendant greeted me in English and asked where I needed to go. I provided him with my hotel's address, and I was relieved to learn he would accept my credit card for payment. He processed the transaction, generated a printed page, and called a porter to take me to my car. The porter insisted on taking my bags, and my back and shoulders thanked him for the help.

"Are you traveling alone?"

I looked around and wondered how I should answer his question, because obviously, I was alone.

"Yes."

He dropped his shoulders and sighed as if to say, "*They never learn.*" Then he spoke so fast it was like his sentences had no pauses or punctuation. "Do not speak to anyone but me. Tell a friend where you are. I am going to take you to your taxi. Do not talk to the driver. Do not get in another car. The address is on this paper. I will give it directly to the driver. Do not go anywhere else. Do not let him take you anywhere else."

We arrived at the car assigned to me. My escort handed the paper to the driver and pointed to the address. The driver nodded to indicate that he understood. I tipped the porter, diminishing my limited supply of cash on hand, and climbed into the back seat wondering what in the hell I'd gotten myself into. I had no cell phone, so I couldn't tell anyone where I was. The good news was that my hotel was at the airport. When I booked it, I checked the map, and it was so close that I could practically walk there.

My driver pulled away from the curb and set off for my hotel. Or so I thought. I started to notice the lights of the airport getting smaller and farther away. I asked the driver, "Do you know where my hotel is?"

"Yes," he replied.

Then I remembered my good-advice-giving friend Lily, who had once hiked through the Himalayas solo; she wisely and presciently warned me: "Avoid asking yes-or-no questions because Indians want to please you and will say yes even when it's a no."

The more he drove, the farther I was from the airport, and I was starting to understand all the warnings. This man was taking me somewhere else. I rephrased my question.

"What is the address of my hotel?"

He replied, "I don't know," but kept driving further from the airport.

I asked him if I could use his phone to call the hotel, and he said, "No, I'm not allowed to use my phone while driving." And he kept driving.

I asked him if he had a map.

"No," and he kept driving. I started to feel frightened, and my chest was tight. It was nearly 2 a.m., and I couldn't call anyone for help. I asked him to pull over while I figured it out, and he answered, "I know a nice hotel."

I was frustrated and snapped back, "I need you to take me to the hotel I paid for."

He said nothing and kept driving. My thoughts raced at lightning speed trying to create a solution as soon as possible.

"OK, take me to the hotel."

At least, if he took me to a place, the car would stop, and I could fight; I could scream or run if there was no hotel, but I needed to stop going away from the airport.

He made a U-turn and said, "I take you to a different, nice hotel near the airport."

The driver had either abducted me; he was lost; or he was on the take, and I'd broken the kindly porter's commandments. Ten minutes later, he turned down a dirt service road through a shanty town of cardboard box houses and trash. People were wandering the streets after two in the morning, and that's never a good sign.

I'd never been in a weirder place in my life. The cab stopped at a commercial building that could have passed for a hotel, but looked more like an apartment building. I walked into the "hotel" lobby at 2:40 a.m., and immediately a semi-circle of five men surrounded me and offered help with my bags. *Like, how are these people even awake right now?* I felt vulnerable, outnumbered, and scared.

This is a woman's fear.

The place was not nice or clean. The "hotel's" desk agent informed me his rooms were fifty U.S. dollars a night, and then I understood the game. The driver was on the take and received kickbacks from this shady operation. So was every dude that asked to help with my bags. My luxury room at the airport was $22 USD. But, Jesus. Maybe that hotel didn't even exist.

I asked the desk agent if I could pay for my room with a credit card, and he said, "We prefer cash." I told him cash was not possible, and he immediately pulled a credit card machine from beneath the counter. He offered to show me the room first, and the taxi driver joined us for the room tour, which was super weird; it activated every nerve in my body and every hair on the back of my neck. The "manager" opened the door into my room but stayed in the hall with the taxi driver while I had a quick look around. It was questionable and odd, but it had a lock.

"Do you have internet?" I asked. He nodded and scribbled the password on a notepad beside the telephone on the bedside table. *A telephone.* I decided to stay. I dropped my bags and returned to the reception desk to pay the extortioner. The cab driver held out his hand for a tip, and I felt so aggravated. I said, "Why should I tip you? You couldn't find my hotel."

He replied, "I brought you to this better one." I gave him 100 rupees. Offended, he demanded more money since he helped me score the luxury suite. I firmly told him, *NO.* I was exhausted and felt shaken from the experience. I had paid too much for the room —way too much. But I understood the racket and hoped that coin was all these bandits were after.

Once I was inside my room with my bags, and the door was locked, I realized there was a window on the interior wall that seemed to have one-way glass, making my room visible to the one beside it. This really freaked me out. I hadn't noticed it when I checked the room out with the manager because the open door covered it. I had Wi-Fi though, so my phone was now online, which was good because the room was super sketchy. I was suspect of everything at that point and wouldn't drink the bottle of water the manager left for me.

I pulled my beach towel out of my bag, laid it over the bed, and planned to sleep with my clothes on. The jackhammer construction outside the exterior window remained constant and nonstop until dawn. The linens were probably not clean. OK, they were not clean. The towel in the bathroom was *damp*. I decided I just needed to get through the next five hours. I slept though, off and on, fully dressed, wrapped in my beach towel.

I woke up and decided to forgo the taxi nonsense and use Uber because at least someone out there in cyberspace would be legit tracking my location. While I was waiting for my car, the hotel operator tried to extort another 500 rupees for my "nice room."

"No."

I felt angry. Everything that happened from the taxi stand to that moment had been very triggering for me. I felt unsafe, surrounded, scared, alone, vulnerable, taken advantage of, used, and manipulated. It reminded me of how it felt when André assaulted me. Why would any man want to feel powerful by making a woman feel powerless, small, or unsafe? That's not real masculine power. Real masculine power protects and strengthens. I felt a lifetime of experiences rising in that moment.

I was standing on the curb with one hundred rupees remaining (about $1) and was approached by multiple men who wanted to give me a ride to the airport.

"No."

The Uber driver arrived and had one job: Follow the route to *Airport Departures* marked on 24'x24' signs along the road. Did he? No. I'm pretty sure he had never been to the airport in his life. He ended up in the parking garage for arrivals at the wrong terminal. One long walk later (with all my bags), and I finally got to the gate for my next flight onward.

I didn't have a chance to explore because it was only a waypoint, but if chaos was a city, its name would be Delhi. Constant honking. Constant. Six lanes of cars in a section made for two. The pollution was the worst I had ever seen (air and litter). The homelessness and poverty was confronting and depressing. Nearly everyone was working me over out of desperation.

My flight to Dehradun was a quick one, and I felt relieved that I was closer to my final destination. I collected my bags and searched for the bank machine shown on the airport map only to discover it was gone. I had no way to get more cash. I tried to arrange an Uber, but it was "cash only" there. I talked to the taxi-stand employees at length, but there were no alternatives.

"If you want a taxi, you need cash." *If it's cash only, and I have no cash, and there's no way to get cash, what the fuck do I do?*

For a moment, I thought crying might be my only option. I sat down on a bench with my bags around me and sent up a prayer.

Please help me. I don't know what to do.

Then, I got either a miracle or another quasi-abduction attempt. A kindly Sikh man wearing a blue and white gingham-checked Oxford shirt and sky blue turban approached me. He heard me talking to the man at the taxi stand and claimed to have a cab and driver who could take me to the bank on the way to Rishikesh, but only if I left with him right away.

I was both suspicious of this offer and hoped it was the divine intervention I had just prayed for. Regardless, it was the only option in front of me, so I agreed. I gave the Sikh man my hotel address in Rishikesh, and he said, and I swear this is true, "This driver is not intelligent. You will have to give him the driving directions from Google as you go."

Huh? Was this for real? Why would a tourist have to tell a professional driver how to get to their destination? I tried my phone, and after several attempts, I realized my mapping apps were not working. How could a taxi driver not have a phone or GPS in their car?

The nice Sikh man called over a few others, and they all stood in a close huddle like a football team and discussed how they were going to give directions to the not-intelligent driver in charge of me for the next hour. It was all so ridiculous.

By some miracle, that driver found a bank and Rishikesh. But I kid you not, on one stretch of road a mile long and straight, he stopped every block to ask pedestrians where to find the hotel. Every single time, he received the same answer. He stopped nine or ten times.

Thankfully, I got a miracled instead of abducted.

I finally arrived at the stop nearest my accommodations. I thanked my driver and tipped him generously. Loaded with luggage, I made my way up the hill from the busy, main road, which was lined with shops, cows, honking vehicles, and pedestrians. Finally I reached the hotel.

Pradeep, the manager of *Shiva Yog Sthal*, wore a navy-blue suit with a crisp, white shirt and greeted me at the door with the warmest smile. As soon as I crossed the threshold, my nervous system settled. My experience stepping into the "hotel" the night before was at the opposite end of the spectrum. This hotel was sophisticated, peaceful, and clean. It was like a complete one-eighty. Everything here was in order. My arrival was expected, and my room was confirmed as prepaid.

I was shown to my beautiful, spacious, tidy, and quiet room, and the porter followed with my luggage. I had arrived a bit early to acclimate before my month of intense yoga study was to begin on the first of March. So this was going to be a short stay of just two nights, but it would be two *luxurious* nights.

It was early evening when I arrived, and I could have settled in, but I was excited to explore a bit and stretch my legs, so I set out for a short walk. Since the sun was setting, and I didn't yet know the area, it would be brief, and I would stay near my hotel.

I made my way back down the hill, and as I turned the corner onto the main street, I ran into a man I recognized immediately as the teacher of the pranic healing course I had just enrolled in. I said, "Oh, hello!" and introduced myself as the future student he had recently accommodated. We shared a laugh about the timing of our meeting and each expressed that we were looking forward to working together at the end of the month.

I continued on and took in the smells, sights, and sounds of the Lakshman Jhula sector of Rishikesh. I walked through streams of air scented with masala chai, incense, and various fried foods. I navigated around cows and their dung and noticed the international variety of people intermixed with saffron-robed men, sari-wrapped women, and travelers in all shapes and sizes. I surveyed the shops and noted the important ones I would need, like the grocer, the pharmacy, and cafes.

February 28

I'm here. I made it. The time has come for me to put aside any and all preconceived notions of what I think will happen. I don't know what I don't know, but trust I am being led to something greater and more fulfilling, with sweetness. In time, all things are revealed. When I pay attention, I see the miracles - a friend when I am in need, a compliment when I'm down, money when it is needed, and divine intervention. I am on the path to healing and purpose. I will not lose hope. I will feel into the fullness of this heart of mine and trust that the Universe rewards the faithful in time.

Just as I was settling in for the night, I received a text from Gio with a photo of a beautiful handmade pizza and the message, "Hope U miss Italian pizza."

* * *

I fell asleep thinking of that sweetness and woke up ready to meet Rishikesh and its sacred river.

Hotel Shiv Yog Sthal sits high on a northern-facing slope just above town and has a restaurant on its top floor that is strictly for guests. When I was researching hotels, a selling feature for this one was a review that mentioned the entire span of the restaurant had sweeping views of the Ganga River, and from its vantage point, you could see the sun rise and set. So this morning, I readied myself and went straight to the restaurant to have my morning coffee and my first view of Rishikesh. I'm an early riser, so the restaurant was empty, which allowed me to secure the only table on the outdoor balcony. I passed through the glass doors and headed straight to the railing to take in the glorious view of the mystical, blue-green ethereal river cutting through the mountains and brushing past crowded developments along its banks.

The river was more beautiful than I expected. The color was otherworldly, and because I'd never seen water that color, I thought it was artificial. *Do they add color to the river?* There was a slight haze in the air that was either pollution or dust; I wasn't sure, but it added to the mysterious quality of the landscape. There were monkeys bouncing from rooftop to rooftop below, and the sound of bells and chanting rose from the temples and the worshippers along the shores.

It's magical.

The restaurant host joined me on the balcony, introduced himself as Vikas, and offered a warm welcome. He pulled a chair from the table for me. Then he went back inside and returned with a place setting and a menu. His smile was wide and bright, and over it, he had the most perfect mustache I had ever seen. He exuded the same warmth and charm as his counterpart in reception.

I like this place.

Vikas asked me where I had traveled from, how long I was staying, and what I had planned for my time in Rishikesh. He smiled with every answer I gave. He excused himself, and I lingered with my coffee in the morning sun while I studied the layout below and planned my route to the river. Another well-dressed smiling man approached my table, introduced himself as the hotel owner, Narendra, and asked if I was enjoying my stay. He was tall and had a quality about him that was hard to define. He had an air of importance with beautiful jeweled rings on his fingers, heavy, oversized designer eyeglasses, and a jet-set style.

"Very much. Your hotel is lovely."

I had the entire eight-seat table and balcony to myself, so I invited him to join me. To my surprise, he took me up on my offer and sat down across from me. We had an hour-long conversation that was *delightful.* And delightful is not a word I use very often, but it was exactly that—*delightful*. I enjoyed Narendra's company. He was the perfect person to introduce me to the flavor of Rishikesh. He conveyed that he wanted nothing more than to create a peaceful refuge for travelers visiting the place he was born and raised.

His love for his culture and community was evident. He was well-spoken and world-traveled. We discussed the United States, India, cultural differences, and the importance of remaining humble, being grateful, staying in service, and heart-centered living. We were instantly friends, and by the end of the conversation, he made me feel I was no longer a guest in his hotel. I was *his special guest.*

He said, "This restaurant is only open to guests, but you are welcome here any time. Please come back to visit."

After my morning coffee with Narendra, I walked to the main road. This time, I turned left, opposite the direction I had traveled the night before. I walked a few blocks in the main road shared by pedestrians, cows, carts, cars, and scooters. It was sunny and warm, and the streets were just starting to fill with vendors peddling everything from fruit to *masala chai* in clay cups.

I reached a curve in the road, and it began to narrow and climb uphill. There was a man ahead of me wearing saffron robes and walking with a bit of a limp. He wore a cloth bag across his slight frame, carried a silver metal pail in his left hand, and gripped a tall wooden staff in his right. I heard him say, in English, "What country are you from?"

I didn't answer because I thought he was talking to himself. How could he be talking to me? He was six feet ahead, and his back was to me. Just as I was passing him, he repeated, a little louder, "What country are you from?"

I turned towards him, and he was looking me in the eyes and smiling with an endearing crooked grin.

"Well?" he waited.

"The United States," I answered.

"Like Obama?" he asked.

"Yes, like Obama," I laughed.

"I like Obama," he continued. "I'm Raju Baba, like Obama. What's your name?"

I introduced myself, and he said, "Now you are going to slow down and walk with me, beautiful Tracie from the United States like Obama."

As we neared the police station on the main road at the gates of Lakshman Jhula, he pointed to a break in the stone wall where a dirt path veered away from the road to the right. It definitely did not look like the tourist route. I thanked him but said, "I'm going to continue on the main road."

He looked at me with his permanent smile, squinted one eye, and said, "No, today you walk with me. This path goes through nature and the trees, and it is good for you because it is your nature."

How could I argue with that? I felt a little Divine nudge, telling me it was OK, so I decided to keep walking with the smiling stranger.

I learned Raju Baba's limp was the result of childhood polio. His skin was dark and weathered. His robes were clean, and his sandaled feet portrayed the miles he had traveled in them. His English was somewhat broken, but I understood most of what he said to me. Some of it, I intuited. Honestly, I couldn't tell if he was crazy or holy. He had a childlike quality about him that was at once disarming and suspect. The path he led me on meandered through traditional ashrams where devotees and pilgrims resided along the Ganga. He introduced me to everyone along the way and was especially excited to introduce me to his younger friends, explaining, "She is from the United States, like Obama. I like Obama," every single time.

We arrived at a bench under a flowering tree unlike any I had ever seen. The tree was full of red flowers as big as my face but no leaves. It was both aflower and still in the barrenness of spring. There was a huge bird that looked like something from a Dr. Seuss book perched in the branches (I later learned it was a great hornbill).

Raju Baba pointed to the bench under this scene and said, "You will sit with me here." He sat down, hung his cloth bag over the bench, leaned his walking stick against the armrest, and placed his pail at his feet. "Sit," he said while patting the empty space to his right.

I was aware of an awkward resistance to being known, but I sat down. Raju Baba looked off into the middle distance and continued speaking to me like he was channeling a divine message, "You need to train your mind. There are too many men in this world who will claim they can teach you about love, but you do not need a teacher to know love. You already know love. It is your nature. You need to discipline your mind and be aware of this."

I couldn't argue with his assessment or message. I still didn't know if he was holy or crazy, but I did trust, with all of my being, that the Universe was always speaking and could use people we least expect as its messengers. Maybe it's a homeless person or a stranger, but the Universe will communicate if you are willing to listen.

After a moment of silence, he said, "You are going to meet Mana. She will be your teacher. Give me your phone."

Inexplicably compliant, I handed him my phone, and he quickly added Mana's name and phone number to my contacts like a tech wizard.

"See Mana. She will teach you how to discipline your mind. You need the right meditation."

We remained on the bench, talking and sharing photos of our families, until we arrived at a natural pause in the conversation, and I decided to continue my walk. I thanked him for his time and advice and, as I was preparing to depart, he held out his hand, and I extended my own to shake his, but instead, he turned my hand palm up and placed a rudraksha necklace in its center.

"This is my gift to you, my beautiful friend."

My eyes filled with tears. It was such a kind gesture. He asked nothing of me. I thanked him, and as he waved me off, he said, "Come back and see me tomorrow Obama! I miss seeing you!"

I laughed because he was telling me that he *missed* seeing me while actually seeing me, and because we had just met. He was wacky, endearing, and the most unlikely friend.

I made no promises.

I continued along the path, which converged with a modern wide and paved promenade that skimmed the Ganga. There were homes and ashrams on either side. Some had high cement and stone walls, and some had iron gates. Monkeys watched from perches overhead and cows—some intimidating with large horns—waited by entries for the food scraps and offerings that came to their bowls regularly. On the right were wide stairs that dropped to the Ganga, but I didn't feel ready to go to the river. Just the sight of it and the people kneeling, bathing, and admiring from along its shores stirred feelings in me. I was oddly emotional and felt grief begin to rise from my stomach to my throat. I decided to turn back for my hotel rather than have a tearful breakdown in public.

For the entire return trip, I tried to contain the emotions that pushed like floodwaters against a failing dam. I went straight to my room, closed the door, and fell to my knees. I have no idea what was coming up from the depths. Since February 7, I had cried more than I had cried my entire life. But I cried. I cried because I could. Because there was no one to tell me not to. No one to hide the truth from. No one to talk me out of my pain. It was here again, and I was feeling it. Maybe it was because I had finally arrived at the place I was moving toward my entire life. Maybe because I didn't expect to arrive brokenhearted, alone, and empty. Maybe I was crying out of relief because I had made it. I don't know what came over me, but I let it pass through me like a storm.

I felt very confused about the space I was in. I couldn't accept violence from a partner, and at the same time, I loved André and was mourning the loss. I understood the tension people felt between staying and leaving. I understood why people stayed.

I showered, made myself a cup of tea, and picked up my phone to check messages. The first thing I saw when I opened my phone was Raju Baba's last entry . . . *Mana*. The contact card he shared connected to Mana's social media page, so I spent a few minutes browsing through her posts and videos. At first blush, it seemed her primary interest was in teaching manifestation and sharing her superior adorableness with the world. She was just about the cutest person I'd ever seen, and I wondered if she was real, or if she was a simulation created by artificial intelligence or modified by layers of filters. She had the rosiest cheeks, skin like porcelain, and wide, brown eyes filled with light and wonder framed by perfectly manicured brows and closely cropped hair that very few can pull off. She had the face of a doll, timeless and without imperfection, but she spoke with the power and presence of a master. I learned she was also a Vedic astrologer who taught Tantra. I was intrigued. Maybe what she had to teach me was a new skin-care regimen. I sent her a message and requested an appointment.

The following morning, I checked out of my hotel and dragged my luggage back to the main road for the half-mile trek to Samadhi Yoga Ashram to check in for my month-long stay to study Hatha and Ashtanga yoga. The main road through Lakshman Jhula was wide enough for two cars and maybe one cow or a single row of pedestrians. All drivers were in a hurry, and I had seen quite a few snarls that left only enough room for a person to slide between a bumper and a building to continue on foot.

The main streets of Rishikesh were cleaned every morning by the shop owners and ashram devotees along their edges. They opened their doors, rolled up their aluminum gates, and spilled onto the streets to clear away dust and dung with rustic brooms and jugs of water before the chaos ensued. There were no sidewalks. All traffic, pedestrians, scooters, cars, buses, and cows passed through the same corridor. During the heat of the day, there was a constant cacophony of horns, which felt like an assault on the senses. I was starting to figure out the rhythm here. Not much seemed to happen before 9 a.m., so I planned to walk this route for necessities during the peace of the early morning.

I arrived at the ashram and was greeted at the front desk by Manisha, a young woman who managed the questions and needs of eight people at once while maintaining an ever-present sweet smile. When it was my turn, she found my registration in a stack of papers and informed me that my room was not yet ready. She asked if I could leave my bags at the stairs and come back in a few hours.

Of course.

Back on the street, a strange cloud cover cast a gray tint through the air. I wasn't sure if this was pollution or mist. It seemed that the entire valley had changed its mood and that it could rain, but it wasn't raining, so I decided to return to the path I had walked with Raju Baba the day before through the trees, past ashrams, under monkeys and strange birds, and around cows. This time, however, I took the stairs down to the Ganga.

The stairs were a city-block wide and created a river-facing stadium for those who wished to sit in reflection. I found a wide-open empty space on the bottom step and sat with my feet in the sand and my eyes on the river. Suddenly and unexpectedly, I began to feel a lump in my throat and tightness in my chest. *Again with the fucking grief?* I felt heavy energy. Maybe it was the residual energy from all who had grieved there, or maybe that's just how big and heavy my own feelings were. Or maybe, just maybe, this river pulled it out of you.

In Hinduism, the Ganga River is referred to as *Maa Ganga* (Mother Ganga) and is the embodiment of Ganga, the mother of humanity, and the goddess of forgiveness and purification.

As I stared into the river, my mind began to flash back to every heartbreak and horror that led me to this moment. I arrived here with a lifetime of unexpressed anguish from a violent and physically abusive father, early childhood sexual abuse at the hands of teenage boys, sexual assault in my teens, cancer, multiple miscarriages, a traumatic pregnancy loss in my fifth month that resulted in a near-death experience and landed me on life support, the failure of my twenty-year marriage, and a devastating relationship with a narcissist that resulted in the loss of home, career, possessions, and my sense of self. I made a yearlong recovery after that relationship only to find myself seated on the banks of the Ganga with another failed relationship under my belt.

Why these lessons? What am I doing wrong?

If Maa Ganga could purify, maybe that's why I was there—to turn all my grief over to the river, to the Mother. I stared into the indescribable mythical haze of the green-blue water, and allowed myself to feel the grief I had carried. That's when the levee broke. The dam was breached. I was flooded with memories from the day that forever changed my life.

In July of 2001, I was a new mother of an eighteen-month-old son who was the light of my life. I was also five months pregnant with what would have been my second child, a baby girl who would be named Isabella. Our little family was vacationing in Florida, and two days into the trip, I fell ill. I began to run a high fever with intense pain, bleeding, and chills. I felt I was in labor. My husband, John, called my high-risk obstetrician who said, "Go immediately to the nearest hospital with an obstetrics department.

Go straight to the labor and delivery floor, give the attending physician my number, and tell him to call me at once."

We called 411 to find the closest hospital with an obstetric unit and were referred to Bon Secours-St Joseph Hospital in Port Charlotte, which was a forty-five-minute drive from where we were staying. We made the trip by car and my condition worsened with each passing minute. I was wracked with indescribable pain and began to fade in and out of consciousness. When we arrived at the hospital, my fever at intake was nearing 105 degrees and climbing. My memory is a bit spotty between arrival and being transferred to a bed, but I do remember the urgency around me and being covered with a cooling blanket, which caused me to shake uncontrollably. I was encircled by a group of people who went straight to work trying to save two lives.

Among the last few memories during the chaos was a man at my side who wasn't dressed like the medical staff. He seemed to be wearing the jumpsuit of a pilot. I understood from the discussions over me that he was with a life flight team that was called to transfer me to another facility. He briefly held my wrist, surveyed the machines I was connected to, and then he apologized to someone and said, "Her pulse is too weak. She won't make the trip."

This statement seemed to create a new level of panic around me. An ultrasound was being performed, and it was then that I heard the doctor say, "There's no heartbeat. We need to evacuate the uterus." I was being transferred to another place, and on the way, in the elevator, I placed my hand on the forearm of the nurse by the gurney and begged her to put me out of my misery.

I was experiencing septic shock caused by an intrauterine infection and the inability to miscarry or deliver due to placenta previa. I remember reaching the other room; my vision began to dim, and all I could see were smears of light above me. I heard the doctor at the foot of the table ask, "Tracie, do you think you can push?" I remember trying to push, but I couldn't feel my body.

The only sign I was actually pushing was the doctor saying, "OK, you're doing it. We're halfway there." Then, he sounded farther and farther away. The noise of the room began to fade. I quickly piled up complication after complication as my body began to shut down, and I started to bleed out. I experienced pulmonary effusion and could no longer breathe. My body was randomly clotting in a rare and serious condition called disseminated intravascular coagulation, and then, cardiac arrest.

I died. I flat-lined.

My next memory was hearing a whooshing sound, and suddenly, I was pain-free. Completely at peace. I was also over my body, watching doctors and nurses attempt to shock it back to life as nurses scrambled to intubate me and order blood.

Suddenly, I was pulled into a long space like a hall or a tunnel lined with columns or pillars that led to the brightest, warmest light I had ever experienced. Lining the hall were all the people I knew in this lifetime that had passed before me. They were so happy to see me arriving and encouraged me toward the light. I moved into the bright, blinding, absorbing light at the end of the tunnel and was consumed by Holy oneness and *knowing*. I intuitively understood that this Divine presence has many names: God, the Central Sun, the Creator. Whatever you call our source, it is the pure energy of unconditional Love.

There was no pain or suffering in the light. No physical form. No male or female. Only Love. Love is the energetic lifeforce. Pain, suffering, feelings, identification, and worldliness are conditions of the body, not the energy that moves it. I was home. I was eternal once more. While I was in the warmth of this love and light, I was without troubles. I remembered who I was.

I was told I had to return. I was told I still had things to accomplish in this lifetime, but I didn't want to return. I wanted to stay there in the safety and warmth of *Love*. I wanted to stay there in that feeling I had always desired but never found. It was

Samadhi. Bliss. Complete absorption. It's hard to explain what I experienced, but it was as though everything was energy, and there was no separation between me and the Divine. There was no darkness. No limitations. No heaviness. I experienced everything all at once and understood how the entirety of Creation works together. I understood how one thought or action creates energetic ripples throughout the Universe, how everything is connected through this Divine energy. But our fear . . . OUR FEAR . . . blocks our heart from accessing this Love; this truth. God is the energy in everything, and that energy is Love. *God is the Universe.*

When it was time to return, I resisted. I wanted to remain in the loving light. I was briefly above another scene—a frustrated doctor near tears (I would later find out this was my cardiologist) was on the phone with his forehead resting in his other hand. He said, "I don't understand why I can't stabilize her heart."

There was a *whooshing* sound, and I felt a vacuum-like pull back to my body.

Then I felt heavy, dense darkness.

I experienced occasional moments of awareness during this mostly unconscious period and thought I was in an underwater coffin. I couldn't see because I couldn't open my eyes for some reason. All I could hear was a sound similar to air flowing through a scuba apparatus, and my lungs were filling and exhaling mechanically to constant humming, dripping, and gurgling sounds. My mind interpreted this as being in a box under water.

When I finally regained consciousness a week later, I didn't understand the thing I was choking on in my throat, so my first instinct was to clear my airway. I yanked the ventilator and feeding tube out with my hands, causing me to gag and gasp, and raise all kinds of alarm and panic around me. I couldn't yet breathe on my own, so the fast-acting nurses quickly intubated me, and I was out again.

Over the next few days, I was moving between unconscious and conscious states. My arms were now restrained to my bedrails, and I allowed the machine to do the breathing for me, thanks to the sage advice my nurse Sharon whispered in my ear, "Don't fight it honey. It's easier if you let it do its thing."

A pacemaker controlled the ticking of my heart. My eyes were swollen and crusted shut; I could not see, and I was unable to verbally communicate due to the ventilator. I was being fed through a tube, and IVs and ports were in every available vein. My husband John was a near constant, and at one point, he explained he was camping on the floor of the waiting room. He said the hospital wouldn't allow our son in the ICU so, initially, he was staying with our only relative in Florida, his great aunt, but our mothers and my sister had arrived and were now helping care for him.

Until that moment, I had never been apart from my son. I wanted nothing more than to hold him, but I couldn't answer questions or express my wishes. When people communicated with me, I could only manage to send tears down my cheeks.

John played music for me through headphones, which was so calming, and my nurses Sharon and Gigi explained everything and talked to me while they did routine things around my bed, but my frustration was growing because I couldn't respond. At some point, Gigi was changing my IV, and I started making a writing gesture with the finger and thumb of my restrained right hand.

She said, "Oh my gosh! Are you trying to tell me you want to write?"

I repeated the movement with exaggerated excitement. *She understands!*

This small gesture was the only way I could convey, *I can hear you. I want to speak.*

She moved about the room for a moment; then she returned to my side and placed a flat object on my lap. She moved my hand and placed it palm down, so I could feel the piece of paper underneath. Then, she placed a writing instrument in my hand. I didn't know whether it was a pen or pencil. I began to write. I would write a question, and she would read it back to me in disbelief.

Can you bring me my baybee?

Please bring me my babee.

I want to see my baby.

Gigi would validate each message, "You want to see your baby?" but her validation was not followed by an answer.

I still have that piece of paper. My writing is so tiny you almost need a magnifying glass to read it. The script runs north, south, east, and west across the page. And my misspelling of baby is inexplicable.

I'm sure no one knew whether I was asking to see my eighteen-month-old son or my stillborn daughter. Truthfully, even today, I don't know either. Perhaps both.

Maybe because my tiny questions found their way to the page from my nearly lifeless body, or maybe because it was the wise thing to do, the hospital's grief counselor suggested to my family that a funeral would provide me with the closure I needed to appropriately process this loss. Unfortunately, it was a decision that had to be made quickly because it was also necessary to handle our baby's remains.

My husband had to make many hard decisions on his own at that time, and we were still fairly young. This was one of the hardest. He later told me this decision haunted him because it was such a horrible reality for me to wake up to.

The grief counselor explained that without this closure, I might struggle with confusion later and believe my child was out there in the world. For instance, I might see a young girl playing in the park and believe it was actually *my* daughter. My family, not wanting me to suffer from unusual delusions, agreed. I think they made the best decision with the information they had. The problem was, this decision was being made before I was fully in this world. I didn't understand what happened to me or my baby. I wasn't conscious enough to understand my experience or to ask questions about it.

I gained consciousness for longer stretches; and the swelling in my eyes was receding, making it possible for me to see little flashes of my room. The first thing I could make out was the crucifix on the wall in front of me. *I'm in a Catholic hospital.* When it was clear I was improving and I could see, things began to move quickly. I remember the nurse telling me my family was going to visit with the priest, and she would bring my baby. I felt a mixture of gratitude, relief, and excitement, but I didn't know if she meant I was going to see my eighteen-month-old son or my new baby. I wanted to see both. Either way, I was going to see a baby!

I remember the strange discomfort I felt being surrounded by my family. Everyone was crying and sad. My body felt stiff, uncooperative, and despondent. I felt frustrated that I couldn't speak. My bed was moved to an upright position, which made the ventilator feel uncomfortable, and I became more aware of the sore on my mouth where the vent had been resting. I could see the faces of the people I loved, but my little boy was not with them. Somehow, in spite of miraculous advancements, modern medicine had created such an awful and lonely experience for the aged, the healing, and the dying.

The priest arrived, introduced himself, blessed me, then stationed himself near the foot of the bed. A woman entered the room holding what I assumed was my baby wrapped in a blanket. As she got closer, she held the baby close to me. I saw a tiny, dead, lifeless baby. I will spare you and me the details, and I won't describe the horror of this reality. I didn't realize that my baby had died until that moment. What mattered was that I wanted to scream but couldn't. I began to cry and choke on the tubes in my throat. I clenched my eyes shut and refused to look at her.

Someone, an unknown woman, leaned into my ear and said, "Tracie, if you get upset, we'll have to take the baby away."

No one meant to traumatize me. I know they thought they were helping, but I immediately understood why babies cry when they enter this world. I had returned to pain and suffering. I couldn't wail. I couldn't ask questions. I couldn't express myself. And the idea was planted into my subconscious that if I got upset, they would take my baby away.

This was my reentry into the world.

I was traumatized and grief stricken. I was also unable to see my son. I returned to a body that had to learn to walk with a brain that suffered from PTSD and memory complications due to oxygen deprivation. I had vocal cord damage (likely because I ripped the vent from my throat), and many, many checkups because I had multiple transfusions of blood and platelets and required ongoing care. And from the day I woke up, I walked in two worlds at once. I didn't lose the knowing or the understanding that I had accessed in the Light.

* * *

One thing was clear. As I sat staring into the reflective waters of the holy river, I realized that I never had a funeral on my own terms. I had never put Isabella to rest literally or figuratively. Also, this life-changing event was the moment in my marriage that caused a fracture that never quite healed. We were forever changed and slowly, in time, we drifted away from each other.

That loss and pain was like my feeling of letting André go. I didn't get to say goodbye on my terms, and the ending was traumatic. I imagined we would die as happy, elderly farmers in Ecuador, enjoying morning coffee in the mountains, overlooking the river.

I need to say goodbye. I need to let him go.

It occurred to me that this would be a good time to turn all the heavy stuff over to the holy Mother.

Just as I had that thought, a woman with a basket of flowers approached me and gestured for me to follow her to the water. She appeared as an old gypsy, with long, layered cotton skirts; her head was covered with a shroud. Her hair was gray, her frame was thin and fine, and her skin looked like the cracked earth of the desert. She had the eyes of a child, and she was missing bottom teeth; that somehow added to her charm.

I was aware she was selling flowers, so I told her, "I don't have any money," which was true.

She shook her head no and smiled, waving me to continue following.

She stopped along the water's edge and motioned for me to join her. She squatted near her basket where she removed a tiny aluminum pie tin and began to assemble a floating offering. She added oil and a piece of cotton formed into a wick, which she lit with a match. She surrounded the flame with flowers and placed it in my hands. She closed her eyes and made a prayer gesture so I understood my task.

I said a prayer: *I release you with love.*

She motioned for me to give it to the river, and I did. With it, I gave all the burdens I didn't need to carry anymore.

I thanked her and regretted that I had nothing to give her though she seemed to understand. I sat there with my feelings for a while. The hazy, gray weather matched my mood.

I left the water, walked up the stairs, and decided to cross the pedestrian bridge to Tapovan on the other side of the river. The bridge was packed with people shoulder to shoulder, and monkeys were leaping around the entrance. Just as I reached the opposite shore and was about to step off the bridge, I looked up and saw a tiny, dead monkey draped over the sign. I felt energy shoot through my body. In a flashback I saw my baby Isabella in the hospital. *She was the same size.* I felt tightness in my chest and began to fight tears while standing in the middle of the crowd.

There were so many people around me. I turned on my heels and started back across the bridge toward the ashram. When I was about halfway across, there was a sudden clearing in the crowd, and I felt a sigh of relief for the space. I lifted my eyes and looked across the break in the sea of people, and there, straight in front of me, was André. Our eyes met and several expressions crossed his face in a moment—surprise, disbelief, and sadness. We stood on that bridge, directly over the Ganga, stopped in our tracks, within a pause that is longer in my memory. His shoulders sank, he looked as though he was going to cry, and muttered, "Of course." He walked closer to me as if he was going to hug me.

I resisted the longing for comfort in that moment and subtly side-stepped, managing to ask, "How are you?"

"I'm OK," he said.

I felt the pounding and ache of my heart and wanted nothing more than to accept his hug and make this suffering go away. Why would the Universe be so cruel as to confront me with both of the things I needed to release within minutes of each other? I looked him in the eyes and said, "Enjoy your day," but what I meant was *I loved you with all my heart and you broke it.* Then, I walked away.

I release you.

The thought of that sweet proposed meeting on the bridge in Venice crossed my mind. It was a stark contrast to this painful encounter of André on the bridge over the Ganga.

I put on sunglasses to mask my tears, went back to the steps of the river, and stared at the flowing water.

I wanted to be alone and invisible. I questioned whether I should have left André. Or if I should have been so cold to him. I was reeling and confused.

Two small boys approached many times asking me to buy flowers. Each time I said, "No thank you," and they walked away only to return a few minutes later and ask again.

Eight to ten people stopped to ask, "Where are you from?" and introduced themselves. A group of men with unusual forehead markings approached, and one of their group introduced himself and asked, "What are you doing here?" It seemed my blond hair, fair skin, and light eyes were a novelty. He asked, "Can I have a picture with you?"

I had never liked being photographed, but I also felt obliged to represent my country well. I agreed and then the group he was with formed a line. Before I knew it, I was taking photos with a dozen men. It was so awkward, and when one of them said, "You're so beautiful," I nearly laughed. I literally felt and looked my worst. My eyes were puffy from crying, and my spirit was broken.

This whole photo-op turned into a spectacle with locals stopping to see what the fuss was around this ordinary, white lady. I had wanted to be left alone on the steps to process all that had just transpired, but as Zoya said later, when I told her what happened, "I guess you weren't meant to be alone in that moment."

Soon enough, I found myself alone again by the river, and my thoughts turned to seeing André on the bridge. It was as if I had seen an apparition. It was like seeing the ghost of my great love with the knowledge he was not real, and I could never touch him or hold him again. Just as my eyes filled with tears, one of the young flower sellers approached and scolded me, "You did it all wrong! You charge 1000 Rupees per photo!"

This made me laugh. This little hustler was giving me pointers on working the situation to my advantage.

I returned to the ashram, collected my books, class schedule, and room key from Manisha, who was still smiling; then I found my quarters.

I had a private room on the third floor with my own bathroom. It was not a luxury hotel, but it wasn't meant to be. I spent what remained of the day organizing my clothes in the wardrobe, the toiletries in the bathroom, and the books in the nightstand. I had a space of my own for the next month—a place to shelter, heal, and strengthen. There was comfort in that, but also, I was so far from home and my support network. I felt that distance from the people I loved. I would have given anything in that moment to hug my son or to be sitting around a table with my friends.

Even though the Universe had shown me I am never *truly* alone, I felt alone in my grief because I was. No one could carry it or feel it for me. No one could experience it with me. This grief and this *letting go* was long overdue. What I turned over to the river was a lifetime of carrying pain in silence. I let go of a pattern of accepting responsibility for the anger and actions of others, which came to a head in my relationship with André. Also, I let go of the pattern of loss—loss of dreams, people, babies, possessions, homes, and self.

We Are All Connected

There were no elevators in the six-story ashram, and the commutes up and down the stairs between the dining hall on the first floor and the classes on the middle and upper floors really added to the experience. Each time I climbed or descended, I passed a dozen different skin tones and as many languages. The variation made me feel less alone, or less like an outsider or "other," and more like another thread in a beautiful tapestry.

Student residents had traveled from around the globe to be in Rishikesh, at Samadhi Yoga Ashram, at exactly that time, and my favorite question was, "How did you end up here?" I found it uncanny that most people I talked to described last-minute changes, re-routes, or rescheduled trips. I heard things like, "I was enrolled in another school, but changed my mind and moved to this one at the last minute," or, "I was supposed to be on this trip last year, but I wasn't able to travel, so I rescheduled." One person told me, "I had reservations at a school on the other side of the river in Tapovan, but when I arrived, they had no room and sent me here."

I too ended up at the ashram due to a change in circumstances. My trip was originally planned for October of the prior year; however, André's Visa complications meant that it was necessary to change plans. So we had postponed for five months, until March. Then, of course, more recently, my own dramatic life change and an intuitive hunch landed me at *Samadhi Yoga Ashram*. So, instead of being enrolled in a program geared towards westernized Vinyasa practice, I found myself in a curriculum with a spiritual focus rooted in the Vedas. The timing might not have seemed curious at face value, but as our teachers advised, this was a powerful and auspicious time to be in Rishikesh.

Two significant holidays fell during our month of residency: Maha Shivaratri, the celebration of Shiva and his example of overcoming darkness and ignorance through consciousness, and Holi, the festival of color, unity, love, and spring.

Guru Vishnu Panigrahi, founder of both Samadhi Yoga Ashram and the adjoining World Peace Yoga School, said, "Yoga programs in Rishikesh are called YTT, which stands for *Yoga Teacher Training*. Here, YTT stands for Your Total Transformation." It was apparent that a rich spiritual life and Vedic principles were important in his vision.

I had a hunch I had ended up in the place I was meant to be all along.

Each day began at 5 a.m. with Sādhanā, a devotional spiritual practice meant to facilitate the surrender of ego to the Divine, and ended with dinner at 7 p.m. I think there were roughly twenty-seven people in my cohort, all of us electing to immerse ourselves in 200 hours of yogic study, which covered physical postures and movement (asana), philosophy, physiology, alignment, anatomy, meditation, pranayama (breathwork), and explorations of Vedic practices like Ayurveda and personal care.

Some groups were staying for just a week; some two weeks; and some longer. There were other educational offerings, such as focused studies in sound healing, energy healing, and Kundalini yoga. There were about seventy student residents in all.

On paper, our schedule appeared ambitious, but there was a two-hour period during the heat of the afternoon set aside for self-study. There was also a bit of free time in the evening, after dinner, but we were advised to spend an hour of that time in reflection along the river.

The entrance gates were closed and locked at 10 p.m., so nightlife was strongly discouraged unless you planned to make it an *all-night* life. Sundays were reserved for elective group outings and free time to explore on our own.

It seemed I was among the oldest residents, if not the oldest, and that realization led to a few self-abasing thoughts like, *I'm too old to be doing this*, which gave way to even more self-limiting beliefs like, *I'm too old to find love again*, and self-loathing judgment like, *I'm a shriveled up raisin surrounded by farm-fresh eggs*. Thankfully, almost as soon as I began to set down this road of thinking, I heard the words of Byron Katie, "*Is it true?*"

No.

These were thoughts. These thoughts were not true. I was experiencing my own agism, my perceived value through a socialized lens of patriarchy, and the fear mongering of my ego, which was threatened by self-awareness and was trying to survive, and therefore, roadblocking my growth.

I still felt very tender and aware of all the unknowns lurking around the edges and waiting for me when this month came to an end. I was managing a calm, smiling exterior, but a sea of wild emotions was just under the surface. Logically, I was aware of the rich experiences I'd had with people since I left André. But the truth was, my preferred method of coping was withdrawal. Being open with others while I was struggling was not comfortable for me. I was ready to let go of my grief and suffering, so I could walk through this world with an open heart again, but I was also aware of, and fighting the pull toward my usual strategy, which was invisibility.

If I were invisible, I wouldn't have to connect with anyone around me or betray my deep feeling heart and sensitive nature. To connect was to be vulnerable. If I were vulnerable with others, I was at risk of falling apart at a time when I was just barely holding myself together.

Self-isolation and invisibility were my coping superpowers in life; they were how I always handled hard seasons, trauma, transitions, and loss. Privately. Inward. Alone. My mother once said, "Tracie, I wish you would talk to me. I never know what you're going through until you're already through it."

She was absolutely right, and this seclusion no longer served me, but it was my comfort zone. Reaching out to others when I was in Ecuador was a first for me. An anomaly. Maybe it was a fluke. My mind wanted me to get back on track and withdraw. Not only would I be invisible, but I would also be avoidant. There was plenty to keep my thoughts occupied, like 200 hours of yoga for instance.

Unfortunately, I started questioning the latter option after my first ninety-minute Ashtanga class.

My Ashtanga instructor, Naveen Mingwal, was a human pretzel that I'm certain could hold a handstand for three hours while giving a lecture. On day one, I realized I had never actually *studied* yoga in my life. I had only learned and practiced westernized fitness yoga. My body felt every bit its age, but I could also feel that my muscles *needed* this practice. It was the hardest class I had ever taken, and it was the first in a series of twenty-five that would continue to build in difficulty and complexity.

Fortunately, I was not alone in my surprise. The seemingly youngest and fittest in our group struggled too, and we all shot each other wide-eyed looks of disbelief and mouthed obscenities. At the end of the class, while lying in Savasana, the final resting pose, I wondered what I had signed up for. Muscles I had used for manual labor for years were suddenly awake and asking, *"What the hell was that?"*

While I lay there, flat on my back, eyes closed, and in shock, self-doubt crept in. I wondered if I could complete this program. I couldn't settle into a state of relaxation. My mind raced through the maze of big decisions and tasks I needed to accomplish in the weeks ahead, like figuring out where I was going to live, how I was going to move, and how to communicate with André. Then, it hit me. I was homeless.

I started to feel that all-too-familiar heat behind my eyes, and tears fell from their outer corners. I was afraid I was going to start sobbing and disrupt the entire room. Then I heard a quiet, calming inner voice say, "Nothing needs to be solved right now. You have a bed, food, and water."

I took a deep breath and softened into gratitude for the breakfast I would soon enjoy. It wasn't a new home, or a solution, but it was something I could celebrate. A meal.

Thank you, Universe.

The ashram provided three communal meals per day and all were Sattvic, which is a type of vegetarian diet prepared according to the 3,000-year-old principals of Ayurveda, the holistic system of medicine based on the ancient Vedas.

The dining hall tables were very low to the ground with floor pillows for seating. The tables were conjoined in a U shape that promoted eye contact and a sense of equality. I took my first breakfast of oatmeal, fruit, and tea to an unoccupied space at one end of the shape. I sat alone and planned to do the same at every meal. I was going to keep to myself. I was going to avoid being asked, "What are you doing here?" or any other question that would reveal my pain. Head down, withdrawn, here to do the work.

Invisible.

At lunch, my plans were foiled by effervescent Uma, an adorable, open-hearted and talkative Bengali woman with a wide, contagious smile. She sat beside me, and introduced herself confidently. Before I knew it, she had completely disarmed me. Her joy was infectious.

Within minutes, we were speaking like long-lost friends with a dozen things in common, including our age, our natural curiosity, and our passion for learning new things. All that and we had recently experienced heartbreak. Like me, she was not there to become a teacher; she was there to deepen her practice after life-changing events.

Two more Indian women sat with us and one of them said, "We love the vibe you two have going on." My party of one had turned into a party of four just like that. For an hour, we shared our meal and energy.

If I had sat alone, I would have missed out on these connections. I would have missed the opportunity to know these women, who were also going through transitions. It was foolish of me to think I was the only one here in pain or feeling lost.

Is that who I want to be? Do I want to be changed by my experience? Do I want to walk around with my heart closed off to others? Do I want to miss out on these nourishing connections? No. I need human connection right now. I need other people. I don't need to go through this alone.

After lunch, students were instructed to dress in white and meet in the practice hall for a welcome ceremony. I returned to my room, showered, and put on the only white dress I owned. Unfortunately, it didn't cover my ankles, which would be taboo if I were leaving the building, as modesty was sacred there. Exposing the abdomen, the center of life, was acceptable, but ankle-length clothing and covering shoulders and cleavage demonstrated respect for local customs. My calf-length dress was all I had, so it had to do. Truthfully, exposing my thick ankles was far from my most radical act in this lifetime.

At the entrance to the hall was a large rangoli symbol on the floor crafted from various brightly colored flower petals. Large, open windows moved the curtains with a light breeze, and ribbons of incense swirled through the air overhead like wandering spirits. Bolster pillow seats were lined up in rows facing a makeshift altar with a central fire being tended by a man who would later become known to me as Mandeep Ji, the ashram's pandit.

From what I could tell, a pandit is a Hindu or Vedic scholar who functions as a sort of priest over spiritual life, facilitating ceremonies and celebrations like Kirtan. Mandeep Bhatt also served as a teacher and Vedic astrologer. He had a look that was both bohemian and holy. He wore an orange, tailored Nehru-collared waistcoat over a print patterned, long-sleeved tunic. His hair and beard were both long and natural. He had a colorful, jewel-toned scarf wrapped in a somewhat casual fashion around his head and jeweled rings on nearly every finger. He was beautiful to take in, and I could understand the inspiration of every pirate and nomadic Gypsy portrayed in print or on film.

He chanted mantras while tending to the flames of the altar fire, and when it seemed everyone was seated and settled, he began a formal Yagna ceremony, an ancient Vedic fire ritual used to invoke blessings, protection, and purification. He made a series of very specific gestures and various offerings to the fire and also to the man seated to his right. Indian students joined in the "call and response" style of his singing, and international students soon followed suit, mimicking or mouthing words they didn't understand. I was witnessing something beautiful with all my senses, and I swear I could feel the energy shifting in that space.

A young woman with long, flowing hair and skirts, carrying an armful of marigold garlands, approached each student and placed a fragrant flower necklace over their head, letting it fall around their neck like a lei of flowers. Mandeep Ji followed, chanting a mantra and blessing each student with the red dot of a Kumkum Tilak placed directly over the Ajna Chakra or "third eye" between the brows.

The Tilak differs from the Bindi, a common brow dot seen adorning married women in India. The Tilak is worn by men and women and is applied using a paste crafted of turmeric and slaked lime. When placed over the Ajna Chakra, it is said to invoke the divine energy of Devi, protecting the student on their journey, facilitating clear vision and discernment of truth.

Another man followed Mandeep, wrapping a consecrated thread of red and yellow cotton several times around each person's wrist, and then tying it off in a knot, creating a simple bracelet known as a Kalava or Mauli. The red of the string is symbolic of Shiva, long life, and protection from evil, while the yellow of the string is said to raise vibration or activate spiritual energy.

The room had transformed into a container for the magic brought to life through this ritual. The beauty of the diverse crowd was unified in white with voices lifted. The incense, the flowers, and the fire all created something holy and stirred feelings of reverence and aliveness in me.

All that had transpired to that point was to invoke the sacred and to ask for our protection and connection. Then, row by row, we were called to the fire to release our intentions, our symbolic offerings to the flames of Agni. We were given a portion of dried flowers and instructed to take a pinch between the first two fingers and the thumb of the right hand, releasing it while singing "Svaha," which, roughly translated, means "I offer." The objective is for the yogi or yogini to release that which is no longer serving them, or some might say, offering what needs to be released. Each time I made my offering to the fire, I focused on my intention.

I release all blocks that prevent me from reaching my highest potential.

Svaha.

Our offerings were followed by a joyous celebration of music and dancing. As much as I wanted to shrink into a wallflower, I surrendered to the energy and succumbed to the happy revelry. The celebration culminated in hugs for all we had just created together.

We had a break after the ceremony ended, and I decided to walk to town to get coffee. Along the way, I noticed a young woman behind me on the street. She was also staying in the ashram. A few blocks farther on, she followed me into the coffee shop. After I placed my order, I turned to ask if she would like to join me.

She was happy that I asked and agreed.

She introduced herself as Anna, and over coffee, she shared that she was meant to be here in Rishikesh with the man she loved, but she had broken up with him during their recent travels after being in a committed relationship for two years. She became a bit emotional while expressing her deep love for him but explained he had mental challenges, which resulted in bad "temper spells," and he refused to take medication for his condition. She had to choose her own well-being, and it was heart-breaking. I was sitting there with this young woman from France, living in the same ashram, and at the same time, recounting a story like my own—a story I hadn't yet shared with anyone here. I was so proud of her for choosing herself at such a young age.

I said, "You're not going to believe this . . ." and I told her why I understood what she was feeling. The two of us sat on the sofa in that cafe and cried together, but we also laughed at the way the Universe conspired to connect us so we wouldn't feel alone in our grief. We both understood what it was like to love a ghost.

March 4
It was my fourth full day at Samadhi Yoga Ashram. I have connected with so many magical people and have some kind of synchronistic connection with each of them. There's Uma, the Indian woman, who is my age, here to deepen her practice and has a similar love of life, travel, and learning. The young French woman whose experience parallels my own, leaving the man she thought was the love of her life because he was dangerous when forgoing mental health treatment.

A gentleman from New Zealand who stepped away from corporate life after facing mortality and began to study Reiki, energy work, and yoga. We talked at length about finding these things after a life-changing event and somehow, in the course of that conversation, we discovered our mutual interest in regenerative agriculture.

I talked at length over lunch with a man from the Netherlands who has an interest in the medicinal plants and indigenous wisdom of the Amazon.

My new friend Will, a man from the UK is on his own journey with meditation and energy work after life-changing events. Cheri, a kind-hearted massage therapist from the U.S., near my age, who put all her possessions in storage and embarked on this soul journey, stepping into the great unknown. Like me, she doesn't know what she will return to.

Today, my effervescent, extroverted, perpetually positive classmate Jess asked if I had found an ATM, and I told her I was happy to guide her to the one I found in nearby Ram Jhula. On our thirty-minute walk, she opened up to me, sharing that prior to this trip, she had ended her romantic relationship after experiencing controlling and abusive behavior. I could feel every heartfelt word she shared. I was so happy I could hold space for her and offer validation. I shared my own recent experience, and we both teared up and hugged; each of us grateful to feel understood. On the walk, we passed the young hustling flower seller, and he joined us, adding the mark of Shiva to our foreheads. The three of us walked toward the busy footbridge, and many curious onlookers stared at the two fair-skinned blondes wearing the mark of Shiva and escorted by a small boy carrying a basket of flowers. That sweet boy stayed with us for the whole walk. I think Ram Dass is right. "We are all just walking each other home."

* * *

We spent our days contorting into impossible postures, sitting silently in meditation, practicing pranayama (breathwork), learning about philosophy and anatomy, and participating in ceremonies and traditions that were foreign to most of us but so nourishing. I had started to find the ashram's structured schedule comforting. I had settled into a routine and self-discipline after weeks of chaos, travel, and disorder.

I woke up at four every morning and started my day with a shower, prayer, and meditation; then I headed to the practice hall for Sādhanā, which started promptly at five. I began to enjoy sitting with someone new at every meal and made a point of staying open to others, making eye contact, and holding space for listening.

This marked the first time in my life that I adopted a vegetarian diet, and while I was sore, stiff, and struggling with the ache in my neck, I was pushing through the discomfort and getting emotionally and physically stronger. I felt mentally sharp, lean, and the healthiest I had ever been. I fought the pull to withdraw and instead slowly stepped into *visibility*. Communal living was ridding me of my loner tendencies. Even when I wanted to be alone, it was unlikely to happen.

During my afternoon self-study breaks each day, I took water, my journal, and a pen to the banks of the river to sit alone and write, but I was never alone. Halfway there, I would see Raju Baba at his usual bench under the flowering tree and sit with him for a while.

I would resume my walk toward the banks and always find Nikhil, the young flower hustler waiting for me in the same spot. I guess he was between eight and nine years old and was one of many street children working as peddlers for the caretaker he referred to as Maa. Maybe it was his real mother, I don't know. I never saw him with an adult, but unlike other children, he was clean, and his clothes were also clean and fit him well, which told me he was receiving some level of care.

I was endeared to this little boy, as his curiosity and mannerisms reminded me of my own son at that age. Every day, he asked me questions about America and my travels, and I was careful to answer him in a way that excited his imagination and gave him hope that he could rise above his station in life, though I could honestly say, I didn't know if that was possible for him. I gave thought to adopting him if he was orphaned or homeless, but how was that a possibility? The person I had to care for was me.

Nikhil was the only child that didn't try to sell me flowers or beg me for money. He just wanted to be in my company, and every day, he walked with me until I reached the stairs and said, "I'm going to write now." He would smile, nod, and move to the opposite end of the stairs, but his eyes never left me, and that was fine with me because I rather liked watching over him.

Every time I sat on the steps by the river to write, I was approached by strangers visiting the Ganga. They were excited to see a Westerner. The curious came in all shapes and sizes, from perfectly plump women in colorful saris and brocade silks to tall, slender, stately men with perfectly sculpted mustaches and beards, dressed in white from head to toe. They asked polite questions about my travels and wanted to know my reasons for visiting India.

After my time at the river, Nikhil would walk halfway to the ashram with me before turning back. I would pass Raju Baba, wave, and say, "Maybe I'll see you tomorrow," to which he would reply, "I miss you, Obama!" Then I would return to the school and resume my classes until dinner. After dinner, I would sometimes go for a walk because I enjoyed the streets at night. The cows were in their sheds and sleeping places. The lights of the shops made all the wares visible from a distance, and people bustled about, heading into the cafes and restaurants.

March 6

Today, I again saw Raju Baba on my walk, and as I was approaching, he exclaimed, "Obama, I missed you!" waving me over. I joined him on the park bench under the flowering tree, and he asked, "Obama, why you not have boyfriend?" And then something came out of my mouth I didn't expect. I said, "Because I am afraid of men."

When I shared this, my eyes filled with tears because I flashed to my last experience with André. Then he said, "No. You must stop this. Are you crying over a boy? Do not cry over a boy!" I agreed with him;

it was time to stop crying over boys. He pulled an orange out of his bag, and I said, "Oh, I brought one too." My orange was actually green, and he said, "Here. You take mine. It's sweet like you." And he ate the green one. There we sat. Many men approached him saying, "Hello, Baba!" but he shooed them away and said, "They are only talking to me because they wish to talk to you."

A trio of teens walked past and saw us talking and said, "That's a fake Baba." And, I thought to myself, how unfortunate it is to see the experiences of people walking by who either want to exploit or judge when what is really beautiful is that two strangers from opposite sides of the globe are eating oranges and connecting through conversation. How many miracles do we miss because we dismiss a person's value? We think the Creator only speaks through the televangelist or the self-proclaimed righteous when actually, the Divine speaks through the pure and open-hearted. We finished our oranges, and he invited me back for tea later, but I told him I wanted to spend time alone at the river and shook his hand. "Goodbye, Obama!" he said as I walked away.

* * *

I left Raju Baba that day and continued on, joined by Nikhil at the usual spot. I anticipated seeing him and had a U.S. one dollar gold coin in my pocket, which I gave to him. His reaction was worth a thousand gold coins. His eyes lit up, and he said, "I can have this?" Then he placed it in his pocket for safekeeping. I hoped this was something he could keep for himself and not give to his Maa because it wasn't a currency of value to her. When we reached the stairs, I watched as he walked straight to his young colleagues to show them the treasure he had in his pocket, but he didn't point to me or tell them where it was from, and I knew why. He had experienced something we all wanted in life.

At that moment, he felt special.

I made my way to the river, but this time, I didn't sit on the stairs to write. I walked the sandy shore and sat on a large rock near the water to reflect on my conversation with Raju Baba.

Should I fear men?

The beach was quite crowded because many people had arrived in Rishikesh to celebrate Maha Shivaratri. A handful of polite people approached and asked if they could take a photo with me. I obliged although I still didn't understand the fuss, and when a small group of relentless, pushy men approached, I declined and ignored them. Undeterred, they stood around me observing me as if I were an odd creature.

The elderly woman who had helped me make an offering to the Ganga during my first visit to the river appeared in front of me with her basket of flowers, looked me in the eyes, and appeared concerned. She was speaking rapidly but didn't speak English, so I was unable to communicate with her or understand her persistence. I felt surrounded, a bit overwhelmed, and wanted to be left in peace.

Seemingly out of nowhere, a tall, broad-shouldered and classically handsome young man with a perfect smile, like Clark Kent, appeared and seemed to be negotiating with the men and calming the woman. Occasionally, he paused, turned to me and smiled; then he returned to his peacekeeping mission. He held up his hands to the men in a "slow down" or "stop" gesture.

They turned their heads toward me at once and nodded as if they understood something. Then, my new hero turned to me and in perfect English said, "I told them you wish to be alone and asked them to leave you." The men nodded and waved before walking away.

The woman selling flowers continued to hover nearby and look me in the eyes. My new translator said, "She saw you crying at the river the other day and wants you to know you can have flowers at no charge. She wants to know why you were crying." I looked at him, pressed my lips together, and held my breath. Then I told him the truth.

"I was crying for the baby I lost and the man I love." He looked at me with such compassion, and his chest and shoulders sank a little, like he lost a third of the air in his lungs. He turned to the woman and repeated what I had told him in Hindi. She looked at me, and my eyes filled with tears for what I had just said out loud. I felt a tear roll down my cheek, and the old woman pushed her paper-like palms gently into my eyelids and pulled them down my face while muttering something like a blessing or a curse.

"She says, 'Stop crying.'"

If only it were that easy. The elderly woman sat in the sand like a sentinel at my feet and said nothing more. She just sat there, taking turns looking at me and then at the river.

The young man introduced himself as Ashish. I thanked him and with sincere gratitude invited him to join me on my rock of contemplation. His presence felt calming and safe. I soon learned that he was nearly the same age as my son, and he was a former professional cricket player and National Team boxer who was on his own personal pilgrimage after leaving his career due to an injury. Soon after leaving his career, the woman he loved ended their relationship.

We sat there on that rock, both of us staring into the river, and found connection in the pain of heartbreak. He told me he was currently on "the road less traveled," a reference to his favorite poet. And when he said this, I began to recite my favorite Robert Frost poem from memory, because he was my favorite poet too.

My new friend seemed to have some type of divine quality, and young children were drawn to him. Several kept approaching us and stamping our faces with a Shiva symbol dipped in turmeric paste. I had three stamps on my forehead and four on my cheeks in no time. Ashish was quite protective, and when people came around to take photos, he sent them away politely, telling them I wished to be alone. Never in a million years would I have thought a very ordinary-looking older woman from the United States would feel like a celebrity, but I had never been to Rishikesh.

Ashish explained, "Many people travel to the Ganga to practice rites, and they've never left their villages or towns before, so they are seeing a white person with blond hair and blue eyes for the first time."

Suddenly, I understood my experience so clearly and welcomed the opportunity to be an ambassador of sorts.

We agreed to stay in touch and walked most of the path back together until I took the fork in the road and returned to the ashram for classes.

In the afternoon, students had traditional Hatha instruction for an hour and a half. I had to unlearn everything I knew about this form of practice, so I felt like a beginner. The instructor, Amit Rana, was a handsome man with perfect English and a serious, almost militant persona. At times in his class, I felt I had reached the limits of my body.

While I was holding *Virabhadrasana Tritiya* (or Warrior 3) pose, he walked by and expressed his displeasure with my posture by tapping my leg into place with a solid block of wood, the way a carpenter might tap a shim into place.

I have an awful nervous affliction that causes me to laugh at inappropriate times, exactly when I'm not supposed to laugh. So when Amit Rama, the super strict instructor, knocked on my leg with a big block of wood, I chuckled a bit but caught myself and suppressed it.

Do Not Laugh. Don't Do It. Do Not Laugh.

On the mat next to me, my classmate Carly witnessed what happened and saw me fighting the urge. Then, *she* began to fight the urge. I don't know if it was the absurdity of being an old white woman holding this bizarre pose, or the fact that there were Hatha police in yoga, or that I had been holding so much in for so long, but I began to quake. I soon erupted in laughter; Carly followed suit, and then our icy instructor broke his stone faced exterior with a laugh that could have been heard around the world.

We might be connected by our grief and pain, but we're also connected in our joy. The human heart has the capacity to be open, generating love and inviting connection, or closed off in a state of disconnection from others, absent of love. The latter could look like anger, rage, self-loathing, jealousy, hate, or other denser feelings. Did I want to live in fear as a result of my experiences, or did I want to continue to walk through this world with my heart aglow?

I had allowed my heart to stay open the tiniest crack since leaving André, and I marveled at the connections I had made with others since that day. Real, supportive people had shown up for me. There is little doubt that we are wired for love and connection.

I choose love.

March 7
Maa Haripriya, a Kundalini teacher, arrived today, and the air seemed to shift with her presence. She is beautiful and mysterious. Feminine and powerful. She led us through our Sādhanā this morning and offered an optional Kundalini Kriya class during our break. I attended, and it was nothing like what I expected. I expected yoga asana, but what I got was a lesson in oneness. After leading us through heart-opening meditation, asana, mantra and pranayama, she asked us to pair up with a partner and mine was Bhawana. We were instructed to look our partner in the eyes and not break eye contact throughout the exercise. She instructed us to place one hand on our heart and the other palm-to-palm with our partner. We began to chant a mantra. Maa said, "You will see others how you see yourself." As I chanted and stared into my partner's eyes, I began to feel an overwhelming feeling of love. It was so powerful that my eyes began to fill with tears, and so did hers. I couldn't believe how beautiful

Bhawana was. We began to sway in rhythm simultaneously and smile at each other. It was as though I was looking in a mirror. Even though she is Indian with cinnamon-colored skin, brown eyes, and long dark hair, I saw myself. Her happiness amplified my own, and when the exercise was over, we hugged and both shared the connection we felt. In that moment, she became my sister.

If we practiced this in our daily lives, there would be no war. No "other."

We are all connected.

Into the Mystic

My sleep was disrupted most nights by a strange, recurring, waking nightmare of sorts, which I called "place disorientation," for lack of a better term. Around one or two in the morning, after many hours of sound sleep, I would slowly rouse from my slumber and have no idea where I was. Sometimes I would wake up and think I was in the home I lived in twenty years ago, but the shadows of the room were incorrect, and then I would experience confusion, thinking, "Where am I?"

In the liminal space between my sleep state and awareness, I would run through the vast list of places I'd slept over the years until I arrived awake and aware in the present moment and consciously recognized I was, in fact, in a bed, in an ashram, in India. I assumed my subconscious was craving consistency or something known and familiar. Somewhere, down deep, I was being confronted with loss of "home" and my desire for a place to put roots in the ground (figuratively and literally).

This erratic sleep cycle had taken a bit of a toll, and I was running on a deficit. Feeling alert after my morning alarm was growing increasingly more difficult.

In preparation for the Hindu festival Maha Shivaratri, students were invited to the ashram's practice hall at 4:45 in the morning for a special Sādhanā ahead of festivities. Rising at 3:45 a.m., even though it was just fifteen minutes earlier than my usual waking time, was a real struggle that morning. I had just fallen asleep after waking at 2 a.m. thinking I was in my bed at home in the mountains. I felt distraught and ungrounded once again, having had the thought *I don't have a home.* For a moment, I felt the pull to stay in bed and go back to sleep, but some deeper wisdom brought me to my senses. I forced myself through my routine begrudgingly.

When I arrived in the hall, the space was completely dark except for a dim light shining up on Maa Haripriya's face. She was seated on the floor, completely still, in a cross-legged lotus position at the front of the room. As my eyes adjusted to the darkness around me, I could make out the silhouettes of others and navigated to an opening on the floor where I rolled out my mat and sat in silence as others filed in. At 4:45, Maa closed and bolted the door so our practice would not be disrupted by latecomers.

I guess there were about thirty of us sitting in complete darkness awaiting instructions. Maa asked us to ensure that we had ample distance around us and explained we were going to be moving wildly and taking up space for the next hour. Then she provided an overview of the five phases of the Osho-inspired dynamic meditation we were going to practice; all of the phases were to be completed in darkness commencing with the sunrise.

The first phase would employ a chaotic breathing technique while pounding fists in the air to induce a state of hyperventilation and hyper-oxygenation followed by an "exploding" phase, which gave the participant permission to scream, cry, or do whatever was needed to express any feelings that surfaced. This would be followed by a period of stomping or jumping with arms raised overhead to embody the experience while chanting a deep, guttural "hoo" sound from the belly. That segment would end abruptly with "freezing" in place for ten minutes of complete stillness to observe the body in meditation, and finally, there would be a celebration incorporating jubilant movement and dancing.

Music that was both sacred and primitive began to play loudly over a speaker system to drown out the sounds and movement of others and to free us from self-conscious limitations. Maa's voice cut through the soundtrack with assistance from a microphone, and she coached us through the first rounds of rapid chaotic nasal breathing, using forceful exhales while pounding our fists up and down in the air. We continued this for ten minutes or maybe longer, and the activity thoroughly excited my nervous system. I began to feel my pulse quicken like my body was moving into "fight or flight." I'm not sure why, but my mind began to race through the times in my life when I didn't have a voice, stuffed down my anger, or couldn't fight back. These events flashed through my mind as if I were experiencing some kind of life review.

The first memory to rise up was my father's attempted strangulation of me around age two; then the sexual abuse by a neighbor when I was five; more sexual abuse by a fifteen-year-old boy when I was eight; being date raped at age seventeen, and the deeply damaging torment, psychological, and emotional impacts of a relationship with a narcissist. When my experiences with André flashed through my mind, I felt a huge upheaval from my stomach into my chest, and I felt a swell of dense and heavy anger that caused me to pound my fists even harder in the air. I began to feel a "fight" response, something I had never afforded myself, and I was simultaneously resisting it, causing the pressure to build and rise into my throat.

When Maa announced we had permission to "explode," I purged it all in the form of a primal scream, along with everyone else in that room. Then I cried, wailed actually; then I screamed again and again. I screamed from the deepest well, and so did everyone else. It sounded like the gates of hell were opened, and in truth, that's exactly what had happened. Everyone in that room released all the pain and suffering they'd been carrying in their bodies for twenty, thirty, forty, maybe fifty years. I screamed out so much stored memory; I swear I could have opened up a portal to another dimension. I screamed with every cell in my body.

After the exploding phase was over, Maa instructed us to begin stomping and jumping, driving our heels into the earth, and sounding a guttural "hoo" mantra to ground our experience and feelings. After ten minutes of that unusually primitive, but strangely empowering exercise, Maa gave the command to "freeze" and remain in complete silence and stillness to witness the body. I stood there, feeling my pounding heart, throbbing veins, sore throat, and a new sense of freedom I had never felt before. I soaked up the peace and nothingness of that moment.

The final phase was a celebration of embodiment, allowing life to flow freely through the body again as joy. We danced as the sun rose over the mountains and soft orange beams began to filter through the curtains, magically illuminating dust suspended in the air. The exercise began in the dark and moved through to the light and lightness. I felt such a profound shift in my mind, body, and energy. I felt clear. It dawned on me that I had never *really* screamed in my life. I had been overpowered and powerless in the face of male abuse, bullying, and violence. This moving meditation had somehow allowed me to face the feelings associated with these heavy events and to experience *fighting back*. I felt released. I felt joy. I felt liberated.

I dropped to a seat on my mat, feeling both exhilarated and empty. I needed a moment to process what I had just experienced. I scanned the room and saw people staring off into the middle distance in a state of disbelief. Some were hugging and others were crying. I made eye contact with one of my younger friends who was also surveying the room. Her eyes were red from crying, but she half smiled at me while mouthing the words, "What the fuck?" *My thoughts exactly.* Why are we not teaching *this* in schools across America? Why are we not wailing and screaming to release our hurt? Why do we keep our anger, rage, pain, and grief held in our bodies where temporary feelings are not meant to be stored?

While my mind and body felt free, my throat felt like I had been drinking a cocktail of nails, sharp glass, and thumbtacks. It was dry and burning as if I had been breathing fire (I guess I was). After class, I attempted to talk to a few friends, but my voice was broken and hoarse.

Without a doubt, those screams were always within me, and I had been waiting my whole life to free them, to punch the air with my fists, to fight back, and to release my silent rage. I just didn't know it.

After rest and reflection, I kept my daily walk and met up with the usual suspects along the way. I saw Raju Baba, sat with him for a while on the bench under the tree; then I carried on and the young flower seller joined me for a stretch until I reached Ashish waiting along the river.

I inundated Ashish with questions about Maha Shivaratri celebrations and Shaivism. When we passed a family gathering on the sandy shores of the Ganga behind one of the many ashrams, I noticed a small child kneeling beside a statue of Nandi, Shiva's trusted ox. She appeared to be whispering into Nandi's ear as if she were sharing a secret. Nandi was placed adjacent to a large Shiva Lingam sculpture, the iconic representation of the sacred union of Shiva and Shakti, to which she then gave an offering of flowers and poured what looked like milk over the stone. Ashish explained Nandi was Shiva's trusted messenger, so it was customary to whisper wishes or prayers intended for Shiva into his ear and to make an offering—usually honey, ghee, and milk. This practice isn't unlike intercessory prayer of the Christian faith in which devotees pray to trusted messengers in the form of saints.

After my walk, Ashish and I parted ways, and I returned to the ashram for a special Satsang with its founder, Yogi Vishnu Panigrahi. Guru Vishnu was handsome with a wide smile and dark, wavy hair that grazed the top of his shoulders. His graying beard was natural, wild, and unruly, which I found charming. He typically wore an orange tunic, and from the waist down, he was wrapped and skirted in the saffron-colored fabric worn by the devout. I was impressed at the ease with which he moved in this close-fitting garment, especially when he sat cross-legged or demonstrated asana. His only adornments were a simple metal band on his finger and the hint of a modest mala around his neck, which he kept under his shirt at most times. If I had to guess, he was very near my age, but he had a special childlike and playful quality about him. He had an energetic *presence*. He didn't engage very much with students, so interactions with him were generally reserved for special ceremonies and classes like the one today. I was told he was a yogi of the Himalayan tradition in the lineage of Agastya Muni, one of seven revered Rishi and a Siddha of Shaivism. I wasn't entirely clear what that meant, but it sounded super important.

To commemorate Maha Shivaratri, Guru Vishnu guided us through an invocation of Shiva, destroyer of darkness. During my practice, I dropped into a deep state of presence that didn't happen every time I meditated.

March 8

Guru Vishnu led us in Satsang and walked us through an invocation of Shiva, destroyer of darkness. During my meditation, in my mind's eye, I envisioned a figure stepping out of complete darkness and slowly taking shape in front of me. It appeared to be Shiva with long, thick, wild hair like my own. His skin was covered with blue-gray ash. He was at once frightening and attractive. He raised a sword and smashed it down on me, cracking my body open to reveal my true self—my energy body. Pure light. I was immediately aware of the ways I suppressed desire in my life—dancing, art, music, love, sexuality. I denied the flow of feeling and expression, and therefore, I denied my true self.

Last week, I was walking to the river when I saw the most beautiful man I had ever seen in my life. I'm not exaggerating. I instantly wanted to know him. He was tall with broad shoulders and wore strange robes. Robes, but not the saffron robes of a Sadhu. His hair hung long, hovering just above his shoulders, and in any other setting, he would have passed as an Indie artist, poet or surfer, but he was along the banks of the sacred river, so he was somehow divine. We made eye contact, and he smiled the most perfect wide smile I had

144

ever seen, and gently, as if in slow motion, he placed one hand over his heart and bowed his head to me as if in reverence. Strong yet gentle. Every cell in my body said, "Speak to him," but I was blushing like a schoolgirl, nodded as a "thank you" in return, and just kept walking. Today, I saw him in my meditation—the embodiment of my desire. The symbol of what I deny myself.

* * *

For most of my life, I suppressed my *true self* and my voice. It was time to be free of self-imposed limitations. I could no longer see the benefit of holding myself back or making myself small. I didn't need to hide to survive. Again, like the meditation with Manari and the boa, I don't know if what I saw was a vision, the product of an active imagination, a message from the Divine, or information bubbling up from my subconscious. Whatever its origins, I was gaining awareness around my patterns and making them conscious.

The rest of that academic day was chock full of hard work as usual. There was no break from Ashtanga or Hatha for the holiday. Students were encouraged to participate in fasting ahead of observances, and many teachers used the auspicious occasion to underscore the importance of their subject matters, be it meditation or philosophy, on the yogi's spiritual life and well-being.

The ashram was planning its own celebration of Maha Shivaratri for students, but I had traveled halfway around the globe; knew I might never return, and really wanted to immerse myself in one of the larger celebrations on the banks of the Ganga.

As a woman, I didn't feel it was a great idea to walk the dimly lit dirt paths to the bustling town center alone at night, so when my new friend, Will the Englishman, mentioned he was going to venture out later, I immediately asked if I could tag along. I was relieved that he was open to having company because in hindsight, I'm so glad I went, and I'm glad I didn't go alone.

Just before sunset, we met for our trek to Ram Jhula to observe Aarti (the lighting of the oil lamps) on the banks of the Ganga at Parmarth Niketan, the largest ashram in Rishikesh.

Nothing in life prepared me for the experience of passing through an Indian marketplace during a high holy day. Shiva devotees had traveled from around the world to celebrate in this place. There were thousands upon thousands of people shoulder-to-shoulder in the streets. Navigating the crowd while attempting to stay within arm's length of my friend was futile. It was pure chaos.

At times, there was so much to take in and process that I felt dizzy, but *it was glorious*. There were beeping scooters, honking motorcycles, leaping monkeys, wayward cows, crowded chai stalls and vendors, all engulfed in a haze of Nag Champa.

Will put effort into standing between me and hazards or remaining one step behind me along the way. Once, I lost sight of him for a moment and thought, *"OK, I'm on my own,"* only to feel his hand gently, just barely, cup my elbow and guide me into a safer opening in front of him along the outer edge of the road. *And there it was again. That gentle gesture of protection, like the one offered by the eldest brother at Mimo's Cafe in London.*

Will and I were fast friends from day one, and I enjoyed our conversations about spirituality, growth, and his perspective of America from across the pond. What I enjoyed most about the time we spent together in class or studying was that he reminded me of my grandfather, just as Morris Clarke had.

In a short time, the Universe had sent many men into my life for contrast, so I could recalibrate and remember what *authentic* masculine power looked like. And it's no accident that this was happening while I was simultaneously bringing awareness to, and healing, my *father wound*.

Except for the cab driver on the take, benevolent, safe masculine energy had been showing up for me since I took the first step on the journey. Sometimes it took the form of a kindly hostel owner, a Sikh problem solver, a magical storyteller, a sophisticated hotelier, a young interpreter, or a goofy Obama-loving Sadhu. And sometimes it was just a reassuring hand under an elbow along the path.

I had lost my way after my marriage to John fell apart. My wound came up for healing and, just like my two-year-old self, I confused toxic, aggressive masculinity with power when, in fact, it was the opposite. These relationships were showing me what I needed to heal. And the Universe was showing me that secure, healed masculinity is grounded, protective, and provides structure and presence so feminine energy can remain wild, free, creative, and in flow. *It is reverent. It's in service. It is a hand over heart with a bowed head.*

I was arriving at a renewed appreciation for the masculine on a holiday that celebrates Shiva's wedding to Parvati. Their sacred union symbolized the merging of the divine masculine and feminine on the night of the dark moon rising—the cusp between winter and spring.

Will and I reached the landmark gate of Parmarth Niketan, which was capped with a magnificent life-sized sculpture depicting Lord Krishna and Arjuna in a chariot being pulled by horses as described in the *Bhagavad Gita*. Adjacent, there was a massive devotional niche featuring the Hindu monkey god Hanuman, who was pulling open the flesh of his chest with his own hands to reveal the eternal and devoted lovers Lord Rama and Devi Sita in his heartspace. In front of these gods were thousands of shoes piled up like offerings, and I realized I had to remove my sandals before entering the ceremony. I briefly wondered what the walk back to Lakshman Jhula would be like without shoes, but I decided to trust I would find them later.

147

This time, I followed Will while he politely carved a path through the dense crowd using an occasional "Excuse me, mate," delivered with a scrappy English accent. He steered us toward the river, and somehow we ended up on the bridge directly in front of the massive fourteen-foot-tall Shiva statue with an incredible view of the ceremony and its esteemed hosts, Swami Chidanand Saraswati, and Sadhvi Bhagawati Saraswati, who were surrounded by musicians, international guests, and hundreds upon hundreds of devotees lining the stairs leading to the holy river. There were flowers, lights, cameras, and red carpets. The sound of drumming and a sea of people chanting in unison, along the water, under a starlit sky, created a sacred energy that sent chills up my spine. I was mesmerized.

Regal Indians lit the diya or oil lamps, but these weren't the lamps I had often seen in ceremonies. These were large, golden lamps with handles shaped as Vasuki, the hooded cobra of Shiva. People approached to receive the Divine and passed a cupped hand through the air over the flame, toward the forehead and over the crown three times. This was a ceremonial act of blessing and purification, symbolizing the victory of light over darkness and a symbol of consciousness, or knowledge over ignorance. A heavy scent of incense filled the air as people descended the stairs to place flowers and tiny oil lamp offerings into the river, all of which floated away like a parade of prayers. The order and unity was a stark contrast to what was happening in the streets just outside these grounds.

The night sky was cool; people were joyful; the water was green and sparkling; the music was transcendent, and I was filled with awe and reverence for all of it.

After the ceremony, we found our shoes, explored the grounds and gardens, joined an immersive sound healing, and witnessed an incredible sacred dance. I still don't have words to describe the experience. The entire evening was absolutely enchanting, but we celebrated a little too late and had to race back to the ashram like two teenagers, through the madness of the streets, arriving minutes before the gates were locked for the night.

I walked quietly up the ashram stairs, like a kid trying to go undetected while her parents slept, slipped into my room, and threw myself onto my bed with abandon. *What is this feeling!? It's freedom. It's joy.*

The following afternoon, I joined a handful of my classmates for a trek to the farthest point beyond Ram Jhula to a spot on the river where locals celebrated Aarti at dusk near the famous "Beatles Ashram." There were no fancy gates or sculptures, no gilded lamps or statues, just a wide open terrace with stairs leading to the river. There was a beautiful hand-knotted carpet in the center where musicians sat playing sitar and drums while grandmothers in saris twirled around them.

On the steps to the river, men with waxed mustaches and colorful turbans sat widely spaced, punctuating the lines of the risers like notes on sheet music. It was a dreamy scene in the orange haze of the setting sun. I stood there watching them dance and sing, and I was overcome with their joy. As soon as I let myself sway, chant, and clap along, an elderly woman grabbed me by the hand and pulled me into their circle, including me in their celebration. She taught me her dance, and I was her eager student.

The quality of light in the sky and on the river, the music, the scent of the air, the texture of the carpet, and the sheen of the fabrics all stirred a feeling in me that I have rarely felt.

I belong here. I am home

I watched the sun set over the Ganga from my nest of new friends, and later that evening, I accepted Narendra's invitation to join him at the restaurant for a special, private dinner party with his friends. I didn't know anyone at the long table but felt included and welcome nonetheless. After the guests departed, I joined Narendra for dessert on the balcony overlooking the city and the river. I could hear the music and chanting rising from the shores while he professed his love for his birthplace, Rishikesh, his family, country, and the Hindu faith. He paused to emphasize his love for the sacred river running through this land and his life. His dream was to create a beautiful, peaceful place for travelers to stay while they experienced Maa Ganga for themselves.

"This is not just a hotel. This is my home." He looked at me, and his expression changed to one of grave importance as he leaned towards me over the table. "You don't need to come to Rishikesh to take a yoga course, or meditation class, or learn spirituality. You just book a room; then walk straight out to Mother Ganga. She called you here. She knows what you need."

Indeed, she does.

I flashed to a brief memory of my own mother, leaning out through the open screen door of the kitchen, in the hazy golden hour of summer, calling to me after I'd wandered too far.

My Mother called me home.

Sometimes, we need to be called home. Sometimes we lose our way, and I had surely lost mine. I needed people, community, and beauty. I needed music, dancing, singing, and fragrance in the air. I needed to come home to myself.

It had been a full and eventful forty-eight hours, and I slept peacefully until my 3 a.m. alarm because, apparently, two days of celebrating weren't enough.

At 3:50 a.m., I joined my fellow residents for an excursion into the Himalayan mountains to Kunjapuri Temple high above Rishikesh. The mountain was revered as a Shakti energy center, and the temple commemorated the place where, according to the Puranas (ancient Hindu texts) the breast of Goddess Sati fell as Shiva carried her lifeless, burned body. We made the hour-long trek in rugged and noisy four-wheel-drive trucks, and several people fell ill as we ascended through scores of switchbacks and hairpin turns. It was not for the weak of heart or stomach.

It was still dark and pre-sunrise when we reached the parking area, and from there, we scaled 300 stairs to the temple. We huddled together in the cold, joined hands, closed our eyes, and coaxed the sun up with our chanting.

Shiva Shiva Shiva Shambho, Shiva Shiva Shiva Shambho Shiva Shiva Shiva Shambho, Shiva Shiva Shiva Shambho Mahādeva Shambho, Mahādeva Shambho.

When we could see the light through our eyelids, we opened our eyes to the sun cresting over mountain peaks, illuminating the valleys below us and the vast landscapes that stretched as far as the eye could see in all directions. At the sight of it, I was instantly transported to my home. For most of three and a half years, I had lived with André in the Cascade Mountains, and every morning, I would wake up before dawn so I could watch the sun rise over the adjacent ridge. I never tired of it.

Standing there, I was filled with love for mountains, but I accepted the reality of my situation.

That life is no longer my life.

I stayed in that moment with the mountain sunrise, wondering if it would be my last, and my eyes filled with tears. I was present to the gratitude and grief and the tension between the two. One of the hardest things I had ever done was leaving a man I loved because I knew I had to love myself more.

I knew I could live without André, but for a moment, I wondered if I could live without the peace and beauty of the mountains. My choices required that I detach from so many things I loved at once and there remained one looming question . . . *Where should I live?*

My friend Jess noticed that I was a bit emotional and asked, "Are you OK?"

"No, actually." I made my way to a nearby stone wall and sat down. She joined me and put her arm around me. Another observant classmate sensed need, and she joined us too. Then another. And another. I don't know what came over me, but these people who barely knew me were about to hear my tearful confession.

"I have no idea what I'm going to do when I leave here. This view, this morning, reminds me of my home in the mountains where I lived with my partner. He assaulted me in February while we were traveling, and I left him. I've been traveling alone ever since. When I return, I have to move out. I love him. I love our home. I love waking up to the mountain sunrise every day. We have been collaborating on work, so I need to figure that out too. We started a farm and project in Ecuador, which was meant to be our future home in the mountains; now that is in question. I have no idea what I am going to do when I leave here. I have no idea who I am or where I belong."

I felt powerless to stop my deep share. I opened my mouth, and it all came spilling out . . . the unknown; my grief over my relationship ending; and my fears about returning and facing André. They listened with tilted heads and watering eyes; then they engulfed me in one big group hug. I was enveloped in a little nest of support on top of that mountain in India. In it, I remembered the way I felt the night before, dancing in the sunset.

The mountains aren't my home. I am my home.

I was definitely feeling wide pendulum swings between joy and grief. But, I was allowing it. I was feeling all of it. Years ago, when I was trying to save my marriage, my therapist, whose name was appropriately Hope, said, "Tracie, you have to feel it to heal it. The more you resist, the more it persists." I took that advice to heart and accepted the consequences of my decision to leave André. I fully felt the heartbreak, so I could honor and release it.

Did I love the mountains? Yes! Did I love the dream I was

building in Ecuador? Yes! Could I love myself more than those things? Also, yes!

The hardest part was trusting it would all be OK.

Later that day, back in Rishikesh, I walked to the marketplace with some friends. Along the way, I was approached by Nikhil, the young flower seller and his friends. I paused for a moment to distribute pieces of foil-wrapped toffee from my pocket. On a tip from Ashish, I began keeping sweets for them, and they no longer asked me for money. Even if I gave them money, they wouldn't get to keep it for themselves. So I gave them something they could keep for themselves and enjoy. Also, their joy brought me joy.

When I rejoined the group, Jess said, "I've never witnessed anyone with energy like you. People are drawn to you, and you help even when you are hurting."

I was so moved by her observation. It hadn't occurred to me that I was experiencing something unique, and I found sudden gratitude for the small exchanges with the children and friends I had made along this riverside path.

As we continued up the road and rounded the corner, I found myself directly in front of André. *Directly*. I stopped, frozen in my tracks. My classmates kept walking, and I became separated from them in the marketplace crowd. There was a moment of disbelief as we started to step toward each other, and when we were face to face, he started to cry, lowering his head saying, "I am so sad."

I could see that he was, and my heart ached for him.

"Do you need a hug?" I asked.

He nodded, and I held him, surrounded by a sea of people. It was a hug of compassion, love, and forgiveness. I couldn't imagine what it was like for him to emerge from the cycle and find his life burned down. I couldn't look at him with anger or hatred, but I could no longer accept the impact of his choices either. He was my teacher, but I had to go on with my life . . . without him.

I started to settle into the softness and familiarity of his chest and shoulders, but something in him snapped, and he pulled away quickly. His face transformed from sad and broken to seething, and he began pointing his finger at my chest saying, "You lost your shit! You left me!"

His behavior felt threatening, and I froze. I was stunned. *I lost my shit?* I didn't even raise my voice that day. Did he have no memory of hurting me?

He continued: "I'm really sad and confused, but you seem to be doing fine."

I looked him in the eyes with resolve and said, "I left you for a good reason. You assaulted me. I can't live with the threat it will happen again, but you are one of the most important people in my life." And that was true. My life was in two parts: before André, and after André.

He composed himself quickly and said, "Never mind." Then he walked away, leaving me standing there bewildered. I suppose that was the ending he needed. He needed to be the one doing the leaving.

I stood there for a moment to get reoriented. I saw that my friends were waiting for me about twenty-five yards ahead, and I rejoined them. When I reached them, I had tears in my eyes and explained, "That was André." They were shocked and had no idea whom I was talking to and assumed it was another friend.

I was trembling from the interaction, and they intuitively organized into a little, protective circle around me. I will never forget what that felt like—the contrast between threat and safety. It was the second time I was in a circle of support that day.

It took hours to shake off the experience with André. If everything happened for a reason, what was the reason? I was halfway through my month's stay and had few answers. The course content was becoming more challenging, and we were beginning to prepare for examinations. I was both exhausted and energized. I was processing grief with glimpses of joy. I had one foot in this world and one in the mystery. I was in a pause between the life behind me and the one ahead of me. I was gradually becoming more alive, and my nervous system was regulated. I was crying less, and my smile was returning. My sleep was improving. I thought less of André and more about how I could take care of myself.

So what did that chance meeting have to teach me? I guess the Universe created this intersection with him to demonstrate the impact on my nervous system and peace. Do I want someone who creates chaos, confusion, dysregulation, and harm to have access to me, or do I want to surround myself with those who are supportive and want the best for me?

The choice seemed so obvious.

I didn't yet have answers to some important questions, but I better understood who should surround me while I figured it out.

March 10

André sent me a text message, apologizing for his reaction. He told me he felt discarded, which is strange unless he truly has no memory of the incident. I sent him a reply explaining my experience that day and told him I love him. "My years with you were the best of my life so far. I wish you peace and happiness. I forgive you. Thank you." And he replied, "I love you too." Then I felt so sad for him. He was dealt such an unfair hand in life and has so much to offer. He sent another text, "I'm sorry." It's the first time he's said it. He said, "I would never hurt you and wish you would believe that," and I replied, "I think the André that loves me would never hurt me. But that's not the André who hurts me. You are the last person I should have needed protection from."

My heart aches for my best friend, but at least I got to say "I love you."

* * *

One of the gifts of my near-death experience was being conscious of the fact that every word with someone could be my last. So, I took comfort in telling him I loved and forgave him.

The predictability my schedule offered was a comfort too. It was a reprieve from the fear of the unknown ahead of me. Day after day, I found presence and purpose in my practice and studies. I ate every meal with my community. I loved my daily walk, like Dorothy on the golden road, picking up one friend at a time. Each afternoon, I followed the dirt path along the Ganga, seeing the same vendors, cows, and monkeys. I sat with Raju Baba for a moment before continuing on, picking up Nikhil, the young stray flower peddler along the way before meeting up with Ashish, then returning for the remainder of my classes. After dinner I would wash my clothes, shower, and fall into bed, exhausted.

There was peace in the predictability.

When the day my young friend Ashish was to leave Rishikesh had finally arrived, I knew I would miss our daily conversations and friendship. He taught me so much about Indian culture and customs. When I met up with him for the last time along the river, I greeted him with a hug, asking, "Are you ready to go home?"

Ashish tilted his head to one side; his eyes became watery; and he shrugged without speaking, which conveyed that he too appreciated our time together. He gave me a small bag and with a half-smile, he gestured for me to open it. Two small, carved, stone statues were inside, one of Nandi, Shiva's Ox, and the other was a Shiva Lingam. I squealed with delight. I couldn't think of a more suitable commemoration of my walks with him. They would be the perfect reminder of the little girl whispering her desires into Nandi's ear on that beautiful, sunny day along the ethereal, green-blue haze of the Ganga.

We spent an hour together discussing our future plans, and I left him with a gift too, my copy of *The Untethered Soul* by Michael A. Singer. I had taken the book to Ecuador and ended up rereading it during my travels. My intention was that Ashish would find peace in its pages since he too was processing loss. We parted with a few tears and one final hug.

I returned to my room in the ashram and placed the statues on my side table. *What should I wish for?* I thought of all that was empty in my life at that moment and everything that was unknown. I leaned in close and whispered my deepest wish into Nandi's ear. I placed calendula flowers as an offering. *It can't hurt.*

During afternoon classes, my mind started its anxious ruminations . . . *Where am I going to live? What happens to my work and everything I had planned? The farm? My investment? What's next? Where do I belong? What's my purpose?*

Hours later, I still couldn't settle, and I decided to go for a walk. Instead of my usual route, I turned right. I went on a mission to find *my* mala, the necklace-like strand of 108 beads (plus one for the guru) used in yogic mantra and devotional prayer practices. My meditation teacher said I should find one that "speaks to me," so I browsed thousands available in the half-mile span of shops along the main road to no avail. I paused on the steps of the river for a bit, watching a group of women taking blessings in the Ganga as the sun sank into the turquoise haze of the water.

On my return trip, I walked into a small gem shop that I didn't remember seeing on the first pass. Two men were behind the counter, and the younger asked if he could help me find anything.

"No, I'm just looking."

"If you need help, my father will read your palm and determine what stone you should wear."

"Really?" I was intrigued.

He continued, "Indians do not buy the stones they want; they buy the stones they need."

His distinguished and aged father, Mr. Gupta, waved me over and pointed to a stool in front of the counter. I sat down, and he asked for my hand, which I stretched out to him. He picked up a magnifying glass and began to study the lines of my palm, wrist, and fingers. He sighed a couple of times, and once he looked up at me, and his eyes seemed to convey, "I'm so sorry." The elder released my hand and began to scribble notes in English on a yellow pad of paper. He then shared his findings.

"You are very grounded with a good heart. It takes a long time for people to forget you after meeting you. You make an impression. You should live in the mountains or by moving water. Moving water is very good for you. You are very far apart in your relationship right now; you need more sweetness. You will travel a lot and work with people. Money will not be a problem for you. You'll be very successful on your own. Writing and expression are important. If you wear yellow sapphire, you will attract a mate with sweetness. Use Rainbow Moonstone to improve the moon of your hand and to make better decisions and have clarity. Wear a star ruby to increase expression."

I don't know if it is because I would have believed anything at that point, or because I have seen the miracles faith provides, but I left there with three stones and one very simple rudraksha seed mala.

It's interesting to think the palms of my hands indicate I should live in the mountains or near moving water because I felt aligned living in the mountains alongside magic animal visitors like bears, cougars, and crows. I love the way water moves through the canyons and the dramatic way the sun rises and sets. Yet, it was entirely possible I might have to leave the little mountain community and the beautiful rivers I had spent so much time near. It's a town of 2,000, so staying there might feel a little too close for comfort at a time when I needed more space from André. I don't know how a palm reader could see all that in little lines, but it was something that felt useful to think about at that moment. *Are mountains and rivers good for me?*

March 14

In my meditation class this morning, our instructor covered the elements of Yoga Nidra, "the psychic sleep," and we experienced the practice. On our backs, with eyes closed, he guided us through the awareness practice by first relaxing the body and calming the mind. He asked us to imagine we were on the steps of a temple. I imagined the mountain temple I always go to in my meditations, a temple filled with light. Then he asked us to see ourselves surrounded by nature, and I was standing outside our mountain home, feeling peace. After pausing for some time there, he said, "Now you see snow-capped mountains," and I was once more at home, in bed with my coffee, watching the sun rise over the snow-covered mountains. He guided us to water and asked us to see the sun rising, and I was instantly transported to a trip I had taken to Mexico with André, reliving the magic of the sky there. Tears began to roll down the sides of my face. A large chunk of my peaceful and happy moments were rooted in experiences with André. Realistically, so were some of the most traumatic. Am I meant to return to the mountains?

There are other mountains.

* * *

It was hard to imagine my place in the world as a woman without a masculine counterpart. I had only spent one year of my life alone. I was coming to terms with the fact that I had spent a large portion of my time chasing validation and worth externally from unhealed men. This was not because all men were unhealed. I was attracting this type of partner from my early childhood wounding, so my subconscious could keep my "not-good-enough" story on repeat until *I healed*. This was the storyline that felt like home to me. Work for love; be perfect; forgive; try harder; don't speak up; and quiet your needs and desires because *if my partner is happy, I'm happy.*

I had lived in a self-sacrificing, self-abandoning loop in work and relationships for five decades, which was common for those of us who did not enjoy safety in our earliest years; We had experienced abuse, harm, and neglect, or were socialized to put the needs, feelings, and opinions of others before our own.

I was also confronted with my deep and real desire to *co-create* with the masculine. I love healthy masculine energy and what it adds to the world. Throughout many relationships, I had touched on great love and co-creation, but I had not had the experience of reciprocity, harmony, or consistency.

In India, I was experiencing reverence for the feminine as a crucial and necessary counterpart to the masculine. In yogic philosophy, both energies exist within a person and one expresses as dominant. With this polarity, the dominant energy can find harmony with its opposite in another.

There was a strong masculine figurehead at the ashram in Guru Vishnu, and he had a feminine counterpart in Maa Haripriya. She was often seen at his side and wore many hats from administration to student counselor. She was an exceptional woman that exuded lifeforce and moved between softness and power effortlessly. She was heart-centered with fierce boundaries, and she commanded attention. She was open and playful but serious and disciplined. I saw her as both angel and dragon, and I loved that she freely embodied all facets of the female experience.

Maa was born to an Indian family in the United Kingdom and returned to India as an adult with a proper English accent. She was always beautifully draped in fine fabrics and took care of her appearance, but she was also wild and untamed. She had a forcefield around her that you could feel and sometimes see. The minute she left classes or stepped into one of the public spaces, she was surrounded by people who wanted to speak with her. I wanted to speak to her. I wanted to have coffee with her and hear all about her personal journey. She led Sādhanā, Kundalini classes, spiritual practices, and taught energy healing courses.

When I learned she was conducting a cacao ceremony, I felt pulled to participate. It seemed like a strange offering in India, but it was the one sacred ceremony I was unable to experience in Ecuador, and the plant's medicinal effects were said to facilitate profound heart healing so I signed up without hesitation.

The ceremony began after sunset, and participants were asked to wear white or light-colored clothing and meet in the event space on the top floor of the annex. I made my way up the stairs, kicked off my shoes into the pile outside the door, and filed inside with fifteen others.

There was a circle of pillows on the dark wood floor and in their center, Maa Haripriya was tending to a fire bowl surrounded by scores of candles, thousands of flower petals, polished crystals, and stones. There were two neat arrays of long-stemmed roses: one white, one red.

Maa sat in meditation over this altar of sorts, and we each took a seat around her. The room looked particularly romantic at night when the brick and earthen walls were warmed by the light of flames. Once everyone was settled, she welcomed us and guided us in a meditation that brought us back to our breath, followed by a heart-opening Kundalini yoga practice. We held hands and chanted to increase the energy. We were asked to write down our intentions for the ceremony: five things we wished to release and five things we wished to attract.

I wish to release:
Anything blocking my intuition
Anything blocking unconditional love
Anything blocking forgiveness
Anything blocking abundance
Anything blocking joy

I wish to attract:
Unconditional love
Abundance
An aligned partner
Lucrative work aligned with purpose
Joy

One by one, we collected a cup of cacao, one white rose, one red rose, then returned to our seats. For the next thirty minutes, as we sang and danced in the circle, I began to feel filled with love, like my heart was wide open. I noticed how beautiful everyone around me was. The women to my right and left each asked for a hug. *Was anyone else hugging?* I felt I was exuding warmth, like my heart was shining light. *A searchlight.* For the first time in my life, I had a sense of how other people experienced me. I felt my own magic but also my power. My power was in my capacity to love. When fear and inhibition were removed, the heart's capacity reached its fullest potential. *I had invited people into my life that prevented me from reaching my fullest potential.*

We placed the petals from the red rose into our piece of paper with all we wanted to release; wrapped it tight, and tossed it into the fire as a message to the subconscious, which understands and thrives on ritualistic symbolism. We were instructed to fold the white rose petals into our page that contained all we wished to attract, and save it to release into the Ganga.

After the ceremony, I walked to the Ganga and placed my prayers for change into her water while my heart was wide open and ready to receive. I returned to my little room, stared at the ceiling for an hour, and reflected on the sudden appearance of mysticism in my life.

So much magic had unfolded since I made the decision, in faith, to continue on this trip alone, especially since arriving here. Each person in my course was extraordinary in their own way, and

162

together, we were healing and co-creating. For the first time in my life, I felt like I belonged. I'd always felt loved, but never like I had found *my people*. The Universe was showing me that my community existed. I had a vibe tribe. The people surrounding me were kind, intuitive, loving, grounded, compassionate, inclusive, and welcoming. Every one of them seemed to be open to the magic of the Divine and the sacred. Each meal in our communal dining hall included a conversation or connection that bettered me in some way. Not one person in this group took more than they gave.

Something special was happening, but I couldn't tell you what it was or why. It was something most of us were tuned to. It was as if we were meant to be there at exactly that time, in that place, with each other.

So many nights I had cried myself to sleep, but since celebrating Maha Shivaratri, I hadn't. I felt aglow with life and fascinated by the magic unfolding around me. I was content with myself, within my community of peers.

The Universe continued to deliver magical connections and on March 17, I met Mana, the teacher that Raju Baba said I needed. I'm not sure what I expected from our first meeting, but I did not expect a mystic. Mana had a beautiful namesake center, *Mana*, along the Ganga. I had passed the building many times and noticed its unique, tall, green, gilded and padlocked doors, but I didn't make the connection to the meditation teacher "Mana" that Raju Baba referred me to.

The building and entrance evoked mystery. It stood out from the other surrounding buildings that were busy with contemporary tiles and signage to attract visitors. It was a minimalistic, earthen structure with a simple hand-painted sign directly on the building to the left of the doors.

Mana

ASTROLOGY

Readings - Manifestation - Tantra Meditations

In front of the center, there was a beautiful tree that I had admired every day on my walks. It appeared older than most of the trees along the river and had roots stretching from the earth to the limbs like a banyan. The small, cement wall encircling it served as a bench for Sadhus and travelers. The tree was adorned with tassels, bells, and ribbons with many earthen oil lamps around its base as if it were a revered deity. Maybe it was.

I was early for my appointment, so I sat in the shade of the tree and awaited Mana's arrival. A cow approached and began nudging me with her head, but I had no food to give, so I rubbed the flat bridge of her nose, and she closed her eyes as if she were falling asleep. Each time I stopped, she opened her eyes and nudged my hand again. I sat there, indebted in service, until I noticed a small group of people enter the open doors of the center. I excused myself and followed the others inside.

Behind the doors of the center, a welcoming courtyard was open to the sky. The beauty and warmth of the space, *the feeling*, was the first thing I noticed. Next I noticed that the structure was built around an existing tree that rose through the first and second floors undisturbed. The interior, earthen walls were washed in a soothing, warm, terra cotta color, and it felt like a safe womb of sorts. The space was supercharged with peace.

I felt a little nervous, as I often do when meeting new people or going into situations that are foreign to me. My thoughts were racing. *What kind of teacher is she? Astrology? What am I supposed to learn from her? What is Tantra?*

Mana greeted me with a wide smile and a hug, and I was instantly disarmed. She had the qualities of an innocent child with wide-eyed wonder. She was like your best girlfriend who listens with her heart and not only with her ears. She conveyed ease and esteem. We sat across from each other on floor pillows, and her assistant brought us tea and fruit.

Mana and I made small talk. I told her where I was from and that I was referred to her by my friend Raju Baba. She shared that she was born and raised in India, and I was surprised to learn she attended UCLA in the States and worked in the film industry. She had been enjoying success, but she kept feeling pulled back to the esoteric, Vedic astrology, and Tantra. And that pull persisted until she answered the call. As her own study began to deepen, she started teaching manifestation and meditation while amassing a respectable global following on social media. She was divinely sweet and feminine, but she also spoke with decisiveness and authority. I felt completely at ease in her space, and she didn't waste time getting straight to work.

She had prepared my astrological chart prior to our appointment based on the date, time, and location of my birth, which I had provided when I initially scheduled. She didn't have my full name, current address, or identifying information. So, with pen and paper in hand, I awaited her findings like a student reporter eager to gather facts. Mana didn't ask me what I wanted to learn or know; she just began speaking and filled the space with so much information, I could hardly keep up.

"Wow, you have a tough chart. The first thing is that I feel you will gain wisdom from Devi Kamakhya, the goddess of desire and love. She will help you answer the question, *What am I really here to do?* This has been a long-standing question for you. Right now, you're meant to detach. You need to release the person you have been in a relationship with. His energy is not good for you.

"When there is fruit on a tree, it must be released when it is ripe. If you pluck it too soon, there is pain. If you focus on your healing, you will complete your karma with this person. You need to find ease in yourself. Wish him well, and release him with love.

165

You're trying to do this professional work with him but—there is another person you should have met in late 2022 or early 2023. An architect. He's the person you should be doing this work with.

"The man you are meant to be with is mature and financially sound, understands beauty, is calm and balanced, and enjoys the finer things in life. He's intuitive and interested in the esoteric. Visualize manifesting him. Within a year's time, he will be in your path again. Another window opens in nine months.

"Clean up the space within you. Cleanse your energy. As wonderful as it might be to have company right now, get pregnant with the idea that this man is coming into your life in nine months. It's better to wait so you're not distracted or stuck when he arrives.

"Did you have a near-death experience or die?

"I see you moving to another country. You do not return to your childhood home. Don't make a plan. Plans don't work for you. Every time you make a plan, it falls apart. Instead, manifest your future. See yourself living in a beautiful place that inspires you, surrounded by nature, and see the healthy relationship that feeds your soul. A lot of blessings from a foreign land. You are going to write. Self-expression is your path.

"Abundance is currently blocked because you're not connecting to your role. Your abundance will be activated when you step into your role. You don't need any more mentors. You don't need more masters. Teach from your experience. Why were you given this journey? Here you are with an abusive boyfriend, and you are still choosing to be a kind human being. Instead of coming from a place of anger, you're coming from a place of love.

"It's important for you to lead spiritually and help others see that light. You are meant to communicate about the darkness human beings create. Your guides are there to assist. You are ready to communicate your story. There's a bigger purpose for going through all of this. You are meant to teach.

"The next eight months should be about connection to the heartspace. You have to face repressed emotion and desires. The more you open your heartspace, the more you will open up to what is meant for you. Most spiritual processes involve people helping each other, which you are doing. People will say, *I can see myself in your story*. Write and abundance will come. Start a blog or write a book. You will curate your own spiritual journey using your own process and your creative energy will *boom*.

"A lot of people are attracted to you because you take people higher. You will teach from your experience and tie everything together. Design your own program for healing and use your energy to help people. You were always doing this work. You're always the one lifting people up. Why not align your desire with your profession? The Universe will support you in this.

"You're trying to do this with your boyfriend, but you need to connect with people who are ready to heal. They do the exercises; they do the work. Do this professionally. Create a process that helps other people.

"You have to be willing to lose what you have now to welcome all that is coming. He is going to come into your life. You need to protect your ideas, your energy, yourself. *Guru* is a very strong word, but it's somewhere in that space. That's where you are. You are not a normal soul. There is no one to tell you it's time to teach. Your guides say you're ready. This is the chart of a master. You have a lot of blessings from your guides and masters. Write about your journey. Write about your near-death experience. Soul purpose is self-expression.

"Visit the meditation caves in Rishikesh. I found a lot of answers to questions there. I feel you will find something there. Stay here in Rishikesh until you have found what you are looking for. There is a huge community of people waiting for you. You will help people heal from conflict and abuse."

She said all this as if it were one sentence. I wrote everything down as she spoke without saying a word to her about my current situation or relationship, or what I had been working on in South America. She seemed to *know*. Something in what she said caused me to think about André in terms of energy. I had to work twice as hard toward my goals with him in my life because his needs were so great, and the impacts of his choices were so damaging, but the rewards had been diminishing. Maybe it was the same for him. Maybe he had to change so much for me that he was not enjoying his life.

I am willing to let him go to create the life I want.

I left this profound meeting with Mana, crossed the street, passed the tree, down the steps, and waded into the river. I whispered to Maa Ganga, *"You can have it all. I am ready to be of service."*

Releasing what I had left in life, which wasn't much, was terrifying. I started to feel a bit overwhelmed at the thought of "nothing" and felt a familiar pressure build in my throat and the saltwater pool in my eyes. I returned to the river steps to sit for a while, and shortly after, a group of Indian mothers and grandmothers surrounded me. They sat up against me, thigh to thigh. One of them took my hand in hers, and a young woman accompanying them said, "They would like to take a photo with you."

For a beautiful moment, I sat there like an ugly, newly hatched bird in a nest of beautiful women wrapped in brightly colored saris draped over the aged, full, and sagging bellies they displayed proudly. These women were teaching me so much without saying a word. They radiated welcoming energy and joy. So why was I sitting there crying over what I had lost? Why was I not joyful to give it up? I knew what I would gain. I stepped into the void. I had no home to return to, no partner, no job, and the future of my two-year project in South America was in doubt. From this nothingness, I was about to create the most beautiful phase of my life. From the belly of experience and wisdom, my new chapter would be birthed.

On my walk back to the ashram, I felt brighter. My heart was open and ready to be of service, and I knew, somewhere, in the future, my healed self was happy, successful, and pulling me forward.

When I reached the bend where I usually sat with Raju Baba, I passed a man who smiled, gave a quick bow of his head, and said, "Beautiful," in English.

It surprised me because I don't see myself as beautiful. I'm rather Midwest ordinary, but I smiled and returned a bow of my head in gratitude. The fact that post-midlife, white mediocrity was exotic in India was somewhat amusing to me.

Moments later, another man was staring as he approached, and when he was a few feet away, he placed his hands in prayer mudra over his heart, bowed his head, and said, "Maharishi."

What the heck in the world? (I had to look up the definition for *maharishi*. It's something akin to a Hindu sage or spiritual teacher). When I reached the steps of the ashram, a classmate stopped me and said, "What's going on? You're glowing!"

Whatever was happening, I felt the energy of it, and it was being reflected back to me. I felt the *shine*. I was leaving my life and baggage behind and stepping *into the mystic*.

I took everything Mana said to heart. This was not the first time a seer, shaman, or sage had told me my purpose was related to writing or expression. There were several before her, not including Mr. Gupta, who had read my palm recently. There was just one problem. I was not a writer. Anytime I heard, "You're meant to write a book," or "You're meant to communicate," I thought to myself, *What would I have to write about? I'm not an expert in anything.* I barely had a voice. But Mana was right; I had life experience, and if there was one thing I had been doing consistently since I was born, it was healing myself.

I resolved to devote myself to serving people and the planet. I didn't enter the program to become a teacher. That wasn't my goal. I wanted to deepen my practice and learn traditional yoga in its birthplace, but I had come to realize that the primary reason I couldn't see myself as a teacher was because I had spent this life, so far, making myself invisible, silent, and unseen. Since arriving here, I had screamed, shared, cried, opened up to others, grieved, and released things that no longer served me. I was stepping into being seen and heard.

Every day thereafter, I went to the empty yoga hall where I wrote and practiced the sequence I would instruct for my group asana examination. I wrote the guided meditation I would facilitate for my peers as well, and I prepared for the exams that would allow me to leave India with the qualifications of a yoga teacher.

I began to work more closely with Haripriya too. On Saturdays and Sundays, I studied energy healing with her and attended every elective kundalini class she offered. I doubted I would ever have the chance to learn from such a remarkable woman again, so I made the most of my proximity.

In the evenings, after dinner, I spent a lot of time reflecting on the meditation I was going to teach as a demonstration of skill for my final exam in the course. The idea of being a teacher, or having something to teach others, eluded me. I am forever a student with an insatiable curiosity and always seeking. The more I learned, the less I knew, which led to more seeking and less knowing, which was a never-ending cycle. Mana said I was ready to teach, *but I didn't feel ready*.

As I neared exams and the end of my stay in the ashram, I saw the students around me leaning into leadership. They were largely comfortable in front of others, and I would say, nearly all came to the course with the skills they needed to teach. They were comfortable being seen and heard. I was not. I was a wallflower, happy behind the scenes. On the few occasions I had spoken in front of people, my voice shook; my hands quaked; my mouth got dry; my eyes watered; and sometimes, I froze. Stage fright, you might say. This had been a big hurdle for me at the ashram, as I practiced teaching asana sequences in Hatha and Ashtanga. My peers understood my fear and had been so supportive and encouraging.

Meditation was the one self-care exercise I wanted to teach. I had found mindfulness practices after my near-death experience and subsequent Post-Traumatic Stress Disorder (PTSD) diagnosis and had developed a consistent practice four years prior in my recovery from narcissistic abuse. No exercise or medication had provided as much benefit as this limb of yoga provided for me. I was so excited to expand my knowledge of meditative practices.

The instructor of the course, Sandeep, was well respected and liked. For me, he was a tough egg to crack. He was at ease with other students and answered their questions, but when I approached, he turned away, didn't make eye contact, and gave me one-word replies. Once, I waited to speak to him after class and watched several others speak in turn. There was laughing and warmth, but as soon as I was in front of him, he looked off into the distance and waited for my question.

"I would like to know if I can teach a meditation that is not on the syllabus for my final exam," I asked.

"Yes," he replied. Nothing more. No questions or curiosity. I thanked him, walked away, and thought about this way longer than I should have. *Did I do or say something to offend him? How could I have offended him? We were literally silent throughout his class.* The more I thought about this, the more I realized I was making meaning where there was none. I felt responsible for his reactions or feelings, and I wanted to be liked. I wanted him to see how much this class meant to me. But he gave me nothing that would feed my "not-good-enough" wound. Probably because he was a wiser teacher than I realized.

This was a wound I had been looking at more closely since examining shadows in my Ecuadorian hostel. I had a need for approval because I didn't trust my abilities, knowledge, or instincts. I didn't trust myself. I thought I needed more teachers and masters because I had not yet arrived at "good enough." My inclination was to seek external validation, and here was a wise man, forcing me to sit with myself. In silence. Who was I when I didn't see myself in others? Who was I without encouragement or approval? *Nobody.*

I had found a helpful technique to game my feelings of insecurity around teaching. Instead of teaching, I was more comfortable in front of my peers when *sharing*. It was easier for me to share something from my heart or experience than to regurgitate from memory. So, instead of teaching, I decided to share. I decided to facilitate the form of meditation that had been so instrumental in my healing, *Tonglen*.

When it was time for me to "share," I felt nervous, and my mouth was dry, but I pushed through. My teacher was in the back of the room, expressionless, with closed eyes. I began to speak, referring to my notes, while my friends encouraged me with nods and soft smiles.

"In 2001, I experienced a traumatic near death experience and woke up on life support. Eleven days later, I began my physical recovery, which was easy compared to the suffering in my mind. It was during this recovery that a therapist introduced me to mindfulness.

"Most meditations are focused on achieving *Samadhi*, but I found one to be very helpful when I was suffering and couldn't silence my thoughts. This meditation transmutes negative feelings into compassion, love, peace, and forgiveness. It's called *Tonglen*.

"The oldest reference to Tonglen is near the end of the tenth century near Bengal. From there, the technique traveled to Tibet where it received its name, which translates roughly to "taking and giving."

"I discovered this practice when I was studying heart coherence and the heart's profound capacity for wisdom and transmutation of energy. For example we can shift grief into gratitude. This method can also help me feel in action in helpless situations. It expands compassion and love. It teaches us that generosity is nourishing. Even if we think we have nothing to give, we can give from the heart."

Script for Meditation Final Exam

Let's begin.
Please close your eyes and settle into a comfortable position.
Allow your body to relax.
Let your breath be easy.
Take a few breaths to settle with a count of four in and six out.
Draw your awareness to your heartspace in the center of your chest.
Let your awareness rest there for a moment.
With each breath, feel the heartspace expand.
And with each exhale, let the heart send out the energy of love.
Breathe into the heart 1-2-3-4 Exhale love 6-5-4-3-2-1
Breathe into the heart 1-2-3-4 Exhale love 6-5-4-3-2-1
Breathe into the heart 1-2-3-4 Exhale love 6-5-4-3-2-1
As you slowly inhale into your heartspace, I want you to think about a person who is suffering or needs healing. Maybe that person is you. Maybe it's someone who is angry, grieving or ill. Allow yourself to feel the darkness and heaviness of what they are experiencing.
Imagine them standing in front of you. See them.
On your next long, slow inhale, I invite you to inhale all of their suffering into your heartspace. Inhale 1-2-3-4
Exhale healing, loving energy to them 6-5-4-3-2-1

Now, imagine others in your community that are experiencing the same suffering. On your next inhale, breathe in all of that suffering into your heartspace 1-2-3-4
Exhale healing, loving energy to them 6-5-4-3-2-1
Now imagine all of the people in this world who are suffering in a similar way. On your next inhale breathe all of that suffering into your heartspace 1-2-3-4
On the exhale, release your loving, healing energy to all who need it. 6-5-4-3-2-1

When the meditation was complete, I noticed a few people had tears streaking their cheeks which told me they reached the place I was guiding them to. Then, there was a small wave of appreciation and I began to tear up too. *I did it.*

Afterwards, many of my classmates approached me, shared their experiences with the meditation and offered hugs. Carly joked, "You should be running this place with that meditation!"

I faced my fear and used my voice. I shared from my experience, as Mana suggested. I pushed through the discomfort and connected others with the practice.

Still, my teacher was silent, but he taught me exactly what I needed to learn. And I think he knew what I needed. I think he refused to participate in my mental construct and intended to teach me that I don't need his, or anyone else's approval.

I walked out of my exam proud of myself and ready to face the other tests ahead of me. I took my notes and books to a nearby sidewalk cafe to study and was probably sitting there for about thirty minutes when I noticed a man in orange robes hobbling along the road with a staff and pail. It took a moment for me to realize it was Raju Baba because he was so far from his usual bench under the tree. I called out to him and waved.

He returned a big, crooked grin and called back, "Obama! I miss you!"

To the confusion of every Indian in the place, I waved him into the cafe. I watched their faces as they tried to understand what was happening. Did this American girl just invite a Sadhu into the cafe and order tea for him?

Waving his hand over my books and papers, he asked, "Obama, what are you doing?"

I explained that I was taking my last exams shortly, and I was studying my notes, "If all goes well, I will graduate."

"Obama, meet me after. We get you Sari like nice Indian girl." *I love that his English is like my Spanish.*

His tea arrived, and he held the china cup in his dark weathered hands while staring out into the street. His expression became vacant, and he began to speak in a stream of consciousness.

"Now you have no need for men who speak of love but have jealousy in their hearts." His statement was a matter of fact as if it had been decided; then he continued, "You are going to Mana's tomorrow to serve food."

Serve food? This was news to me. *Serve food for what?* But, I knew better than to question Raju Baba at that point.

"OK, I'll be there tomorrow. And I'll meet you after my exams are finished today."

He gathered up his cloth bag, his staff and pail, and then walked off waving "Bye Obama, I miss you!"

Later that day, with shaking knees and voice, I managed to stand in front of my peers and complete my exams teaching a hatha class and presenting one asana with alignment. Perfect? No. Progress for me? Yes.

I did it.

I completed my 200 hours and passed all of my exams. I had also completed energy healing coursework with Haripriya. Still, I had a persistent, aching feeling that I was not done in India. I wasn't ready to leave. I hadn't reached the top of the mountain yet.

After my exams, I found Raju Baba sitting on the bench under the flowering tree, eager to go on a mission. He led the way and walked surprisingly fast. We stopped at a chai stand and sat on temple stairs toasting with clay cups. Then we carried on, and he led the way to a large fabric store just outside the gates of Parmarth Niketan. There was every type of fabric you could imagine, from floor to ceiling, and dozens of shopkeepers were there to assist. As I browsed through the bolts and stacks, one caught my eye at the very bottom of the last row. It had a triangle print with a small, beaded band on its edge. Baba translated, and, I have to say, the shopkeepers were completely and thoroughly confused. *What is this man doing shopping with this pale woman?* There was a lot of stirring and narrowing of the eyes. I didn't care. I was in a state of wonder to be having the experience. Baba explained that I had to have a *kurta* made to wear under my sari. I was a little confused, so I just followed his lead. I bought five to six meters of orange, cotton fabric, the color of the devout and one of two colors that reminded me of Rishikesh; the other was the unmistakable color of the river. Once I had a sari and fabric, Raju Baba said, "Now, we will go."

I followed him once more, with no idea where we were heading, this time through the gates of Parmarth Niketan which I had only previously experienced at night. The place was its own walled city equipped with apartments, shops, and children playing games in courtyards. If I wasn't with Raju Baba, I would have been disoriented by the series of turns through passages and doorways that reminded me of Venice.

He stopped near the gates on the opposite side of the compound and paused at a non-descript door that had no signage or markings. He knocked, and a young man opened the door to reveal a small room with stacks of fabric covering the floor and shelves lining three of the walls. There were several low tables and old sewing machines surrounded by spools of thread. There was an iron I would estimate to be half a century old that was held together by tape and wire near a stack of kurtas on an ironing board in the center of the room. *Ahh, this is the tailor.*

There was real confusion on this young man's face, and he immediately started expressing to Baba that my presence called for the man in charge. Baba explained, "He's going to get his grandfather." Fifteen minutes later, the young man returned with his grandfather, who was probably in his late seventies, perpetually annoyed, and short on time. He entered in the same hurry he applied to his task, and he didn't mess around. He grabbed a tape measure and began to assess every possible angle of my form like a structural engineer assessing an aggravating problem. He took some measurements twice with sighs (*sighs for size*) writing them all down with ink in the corner of the orange fabric I bought at the market.

The tailor asked me questions through Baba, "How long does she want it? Long sleeves or short sleeves?"

Baba replied in Hindi and then explained in English, "I told him it must cover your knees. You want long sleeve or short sleeve?"

For a moment, I thought this was a silly question because it was ninety degrees and I was sweating bullets.

"Short sleeves please."

I have a confession to make. The joy this experience brought me was indescribable—being inside the hidden world of the locals. Standing in a room filled with fabric, scraps, patterns, threads, and machines that had been operating for nearly a century, while being fitted for clothing that would be made for me, for my body. Because the space was too small to hold all of us, Raju Baba stood in the doorway like a sentinel the entire time, and served as a bridge between two worlds like some kind of eccentric fairy Godfather preparing me for a ball.

The grumpy elder grumbled something in Hindi, and Raju Baba said, "They will be ready in two days."

Off we went, back the way we came, and I left Baba at his bench under the flowering tree. As I was walking away he said, "Bye Obama! I miss you!"

On my return walk, the sun was setting over the Ganga, and it was especially surreal, so I made my way to the beach and sat on the big rock I had once shared with my young friend Ashish. A wandering Brahman bull walked into the scene just feet from where I was sitting, and the setting sun aligned perfectly with its hump. As I was taking a picture, I heard a voice, "Do you wish to be alone?"

In that moment, the Universe delivered a new friend, Sri, a celibate monk, who had relocated to the warmth of Rishikesh for health reasons. He was far from the Himalayan mountain cave he called home. Having never met a monk who lived in a cave, I invited him to sit on the rock with me. Together, we watched the sun set over the cow's hump and shared photos of our mountain homes, both of us wondering if we would ever return to the places we loved, and each of us was better for the other's company for a while.

I listened to his life story, and he asked questions about my life in America. Our chance meeting offered a point where our two life paths converged.

Each of us was now part of the other's story.

On the return trip to the ashram, I felt so much gratitude for the lessons and experiences the Universe had given me. The only problem with stepping into the flow of the mystic Universe is this —the unknown becomes more attractive than the familiar. Once you experience the magic, you can't settle for the ordinary.

Digging in the Dirt

March 24

Today is an auspicious day. The date is 3/24/24. It is a full moon. It is the night Hindus celebrate Holika, and the shores of the Ganga are burning with fires. It is also a lunar eclipse and the day I graduated from my course. I can now register as an Ashtanga and Hatha teacher in the U.S.

* * *

Our graduation ceremony was as beautiful as the opening ceremony with most of the same elements, flowers, fire, and chanting, but it was different in one significant way; we were not only unified in white, but by our shared experiences and close friendships, which made it difficult to say *goodbye.* I let myself fully experience the joy of the moment with the people I had come to love. Soon, we would leave the ashram and return to our homes to integrate the lessons of the month. There was hugging, tears, dancing, laughter, and joy. But also, sadness was building, especially in me. I didn't feel ready to leave. I thought of Mana's guidance—"Stay here in Rishikesh until you have found what you are looking for."

There were questions I had not yet answered. *Where am I going to live when I return to Washington? Should I stay in the mountains? Should I return to my home state of Ohio? Should I start over somewhere else?*

I still had one week to answer these questions and a few important things ahead of me that might help me arrive at a conclusion.

After the graduation ceremony, I walked the river path and arrived at Mana's to "help serve food" per Raju Baba's instructions. The center's doors were closed, so I sat under the beautiful old tree which was adorned with tassels and garlands in front of the building. I could see the mystical river and, while I lacked answers, I also felt a sense of accomplishment. I had completed the program. I broke through my fears; I made the trip; I passed my exams; but I didn't yet have the next step. I felt a little wave of sadness wash over me. I felt alone.

I closed my eyes and heard that inner voice, *Nothing has to be solved right now.*

Mostly, my mind was clear and free of thoughts. I was present and at peace, but the nothingness was interrupted by the mental flash of an image. The image of a bumper sticker.

In the midwestern states (maybe elsewhere), it's common to see cars with a bold, yellow sticker that reads "STUDENT DRIVER." This sticker lets everyone know to be patient because the car is operated by a new driver. So, what about the human heart? Why don't we wear a big sticker over our chest that says "LEARNING."

What else would mine say? *Be patient with me. I've been hurt. I'm scared. It's not easy for me to trust. I need help taking down these walls. I feel undeserving. I'm not good enough.*

It would be OK to admit these things because we all know what learning is like. Learning something new. Like a language. We all know what it's like to go out into the world, risk ourselves in love, take chances, or face fears, so we can break through what's holding us back.

I thought about this while I was sitting under that beautiful tree and feeling grateful for my lifetime of *LEARNING*. The continued *LEARNING*. A puppy curled up next to me and fell asleep, and I was grateful that he felt safe. Then my favorite calf approached and put its head on my lap, and she fell asleep too. I sat there under that tree with a puppy and calf for almost two hours that passed in what seemed like minutes.

When Mana arrived, I joined her family and friends in the courtyard. I was so happy to be in her presence again, and I greeted her with a warm hug. I felt a sisterhood with her that I can't explain. She and her staff prepared food to give to the community as *Prasad*, an offering.

According to Mana, in giving, one receives more than they give, and being present to witness her practice was truly heart opening. At first, I observed as she set up just outside the center doors and began offering fruit to people who passed. Sadhus, homeless people, locals, and tourists—all accepted the gift with sincere gratitude.

Mana invited me to join in the distribution and made space for me among her volunteers. Immediately, I understood why she did this. I could see the lessons of the past month present in the practice of Prasad. Making space for others at the table helps people feel seen and included. Giving allows others to connect with gratitude, and in that gratitude, the giver generates more gratitude. It's an amplification. Also, like my first Kundalini experience, I could see myself in the faces of others. Appreciation for my own abundance made me want to do and give more, just as Tonglen meditation reminded me that when I think I have nothing to give, I have love. When I have more than enough for myself, I can share my abundance with others. The Universe operates in reciprocity and offers no benefit for selfish hoarding.

I felt honored to have been included in Mana's personal world for a moment. Prasad was a *lesson and a blessin'.*

After the food ran out, I joined Mana on the floor of her earthen studio for tea, and we talked like long-lost, best friends for hours. Her husband patiently waited for us to tire of each other, so he could return home.

I admitted that I felt sad and conflicted about leaving Rishikesh, but since I would be around for another week, we planned to meet for tea and girl talk one more time before my departure.

I returned to the Ashram, packed my bags, and then met my classmates at a nearby juice bar for one last celebration. Afterwards, I walked along the beach to see the massive bonfires of *Holika*

Duhan burning along the banks of the Ganga under the full moon on the eve of Holi. These fires are a symbolic celebration of the triumph of good over evil, specifically, the legend of Holika and Prahlada. I thought of the things I was willing to let burn and all of the ways I was prevailing.

Standing there on Maa Ganga's soft, sandy shoulders, I had a strong feeling I was meant to stay in India a little longer.

How?

The following morning, everyone in the ashram assembled on the rooftop overlook, wearing white, to kick off the celebration of Holi, the festival of color that celebrates the Divine love of Radha and Krishna and commemorates renewal and the arrival of spring. Holi is celebrated through childlike play. People throw water at each other and smear colorful *gulal* powders on the skin of everyone they meet or pass on the street. My first experiences with this tradition were gentle. Classmates threw vibrant colored powders on my shirt and dusted the top of my head. The owner of the coffee shop asked if he could place color on my face before painting blue stripes across my cheeks. Even his dog had a nice smear of red down her snout. A random stranger on the street stopped me and asked if he could place a dot on my brow.

Once we were properly powdered and soaked, Guru Vishnu led us in a parade to the ashram of his friend, the "Iron Baba," on the banks of the river where we celebrated with song. At one point, our Guru climbed atop his friend's table and began singing and dancing. It was one of the most special things I had ever observed. It's rare to see an adult so free in their joy, uninhibited, and unafraid of judgment. For me, it represented complete liberation. In witnessing it, I recognized that I wasn't there yet. I was still holding myself back.

From there, Maa Haripriya guided us to the shore, and we held hands and waded into the river to wash away the color. The Ganga was cold and invigorating, and it marked the first time I fully submerged and swam in the water. I felt purified on so many levels.

Afterward, we sat in a circle on the sand with Guru Vishnu while the sun warmed us and sparkled on the surface of the moving water. He explained the importance of play and joy in our lives. I thought about the messages I received from my Father around joy. Play was dangerous. I was ready to confront that too.

I was a new, blank slate, but on the return walk, my experience of the celebration became somewhat darker. The streets were filled with visitors who had arrived to celebrate the holiday in Rishikesh. Between the banks of the river and the ashram, I was touched by scores of strangers eager to paint me with color. They meant no harm, but I felt unprepared for that level of touch. By the time I reached my room, every square inch of my exposed skin was saturated with color. I showered and washed my hair several times to remove the chalk-like pigments.

The experience allowed me to examine a full range of feelings between consent and invasiveness. It allowed me to experience the ease of playfulness and what happens when I am not able to hold my boundaries.

Throughout the remainder of the day, I said tearful goodbyes to my friends and wished them well on their journeys. I packed my bags and made my own departure, passing through a vacant lobby without fanfare. I transferred my luggage to my favorite hotel along a back road to avoid the wild chaos of the streets. I felt such sadness leaving the ashram. It didn't feel right.

As soon as I reached the steps of the hotel, Pradeep was there in his sharp suit, holding the door open, aglow with a warm smile that instantly turned me to melted butter. If there was one place in this world that felt like a monument to Divine, safe masculine energy, this was it for me.

Nearly every time I entered or exited the hotel, a kindly man was fixed in the corner of the lobby with his hands folded peacefully in his lap over an old book; or sometimes, he was reading a newspaper. He had a distinguished look about him like a bohemian priest. He wore a long kurta, tailored nero-collared vest, small round cap, layers of necklaces and rings on many of his fingers. Every time he saw me, his face lit up, and he smiled, but I was aware he did not speak English. He often bowed his head to me, and I instinctively returned the gesture.

After I settled into my room, I went to the restaurant and was happy to see Vikas once more.

"How long will you be staying with us ma'am?"

"Until my departure on April 2."

"Very good."

I ordered ginger-lemon-honey tea and soon after it arrived, Narendra joined me on the balcony. He said, "Tracie, so good to have you back. How are you today? You look as though you have something on your mind."

I invited him to join me and confessed I was sad to be leaving. I felt pulled to stay in Rishikesh. I had not told Narendra my reasons for traveling alone. I had not yet shared my heartbreak with him and didn't know if I wanted to.

"I feel conflicted about leaving Rishikesh. I ended a relationship at the start of this trip, and I need to make important decisions before I return home."

Narendra said, "Oh, well you must speak with my astrologer."

"You have a personal astrologer?"

"Yes, H.N. Kukreti. He is in the lobby. I will arrange for a meeting and a translator."

"You mean the man who sits in the corner of the lobby reading every day? He is your astrologer?"

"Yes. He is a very good astrologer and advisor. He will help you understand this transition."

I had already received such valuable insight from Mana, but I was also grateful for Narendra's referral, and I couldn't refuse the offer to speak with the mystic in the lobby.

The following morning, I returned to the ashram for a one-on-one healing session with Maa Haripriya. I had completed energy healing coursework with her but wanted to experience her healing abilities first hand.

It was so strange to enter the ashram and find it deserted and quiet. The ever-smiling Manisha was at the front desk, and it was the first time I'd ever seen her alone. She was typically fielding questions from at least five people while shuffling papers and directing staff.

She informed me that Haripriya was waiting for me in the healing arts center on the third floor, so I walked up the stairs, past the room I had checked out of the day before, and found Maa waiting in a small, dimly lit office. There was one window covered with heavy curtains that blocked the sunlight. There was no furniture in the room that I can recall. After exchanging hugs and pleasantries, she invited me to lie on a floor mat.

She guided me through a breath and grounding practice and explained her process while kneeling on the floor beside me.

"I am going to begin by asking you the age you are now and I will slowly walk you backwards through your life. I will ask you to visit an age and give me one word that describes that year. I will be applying pressure and massaging your abdomen as we go. Do you understand?"

"Yes."

After guiding me through additional breathing and visualization, with my eyes closed, she began.

"How old are you?"

"Fifty-three."

While she was kneading my stomach, she began asking questions.

"Using one word, describe fifty-one"
Awakening
"Forty-nine."
Black.
"Forty."
Confused.
"Thirty."
Joy.
"Twenty"
Hopeful.
"Seventeen."
Lost.
"Twelve."
Misunderstood.
"Seven."
Scared.

I realized through this exercise how many dark, painful years I'd lived through with the most joyous being the year my son was born. Throughout my life, I had been happy, but also, I had survived and endured so much.

She began to speak while continuing to knead my abdomen with both her hands and said, "There are three souls that require healing. The first is your mother."

I was confused. Why would my mother need healing?

"Tell her you forgive her for being too afraid to leave. "Say, 'I forgive you for being too afraid to leave.'"

I really didn't understand. I love my mother and couldn't identify any ill feelings I harbored. But, I could see her clearly in my mind. She was so young when she had me. Only nineteen. So terrorized by my Father. So afraid. I remember watching him try to kill her too. I felt such compassion for her. I didn't need to forgive her, but I could see that she carried guilt and remorse. She needed to know she was forgiven.

I forgive you for being too afraid to leave.

"Tell her you forgive her for not knowing any better. Tell her she did her best."

I forgive you for not knowing any better. You did your best.

"What color is your Mother's soul?"

Green.

"Offer the green soul love and compassion."

I felt it. I felt my heart soften so completely for her. I wanted her to feel forgiven, and loved, and to know compassion.

Maa continued.

"There's a second soul that needs healing."

She began pushing harder into my stomach, and I could feel a knot buried deep.

"It's your Father. Go to the moment he took your breath away."

I knew exactly what she was talking about. *That day.* The day I learned silence and invisibility were necessary for my survival. How did she know this? I felt my upper lip stiffen. My stomach tightened. Tears streamed down my face.

"Forgive him for trying to kill you."

Holy hell. Can I do this? Can I forgive my Father for strangling me? For trying to kill me? For years of his violence which required my silence? It occurred to me. This forgiveness was my price of freedom. It was so *I* could be free. It allowed me control, and I set the terms of the agreement. If I freed him with forgiveness, he no longer occupied this space in my life as a tormenter.

"Forgive him for trying to kill you."

I forgive you for trying to kill me.

"Forgive him for being mentally ill."

I forgive you for being mentally ill.

"Forgive him for not knowing any better."

I forgive you for not knowing any better.

191

What happened next was so unconventional and confronting. She straddled my legs and pushed deeply into my belly saying "We're going to scream it out—the scream you couldn't release when his hands were around your throat. Take a deep breath. Are you ready?"

I took a deep breath, and as I exhaled, she pushed deep into the knot in my belly.

I couldn't scream.

She pushed harder.

"Scream Tracie."

Something was immobilizing my breath, chest, and voice.

"We're going to scream together, on three. One, two, three."

On the count of three I screamed from the pit in my stomach, and she screamed with me. We screamed like banshees while she pushed deep into my gut.

"Again!"

I screamed again and began to sob like the scared two-year-old child I was the day my father tried to kill me.

"Again!"

I drew a deep breath and screamed until I had nothing left to release but tears.

Haripriya's voice softened to that of a gentle mother, "OK my angel. I need you to see your Father. Can you see him?"

Yes.

"What color is his soul?"

Black.

"Can you send this black soul love and compassion?"

Yes.

"There is another soul here that needs healing. This is someone who broke you."

I knew who she was talking about. This was my most shameful chapter. This was the marriage I didn't like to acknowledge. The black years of my life. My second husband, Mitch. I met him at a vulnerable time in my life, and I had a big gaping wound after the collapse of my twenty-two-year relationship with John.

Mitch brought fun into my life. Adventure. He showered me with attention. When he began to talk about marriage, my intuition was "no." Something made me feel unsure and resistant. I had a feeling he wasn't what he seemed.

Occasionally, I would see a bitterness in him or a random temper flare-up that was incongruent. But I kept focusing on the fun he added to my life and his good qualities. I overlooked conspicuous red flags.

When I resisted the idea of marriage, he would tell me I was letting fear rule my life, and I considered he might be right about that. I began to doubt my intuition and I began thinking maybe it was fear. Maybe I was afraid of going all in. So, I softened. I began to plan a life with him. A year after we met, he proposed, and a year after that, we married.

On the very night we married, the *very night*, his feelings for me changed. We didn't consummate our marriage that evening, and I was bewildered but brushed it off and excused his behavior. After all, *It was a big day*.

From that day forward, he became cold, and his affection was intermittent although his praise and attention was effusive in public view. And so began the complicated and hard-to-see abuse of a narcissist. For the years that followed, I fell into a pattern of pleasing, self-sacrificing, and workaholism to earn breadcrumbs of love and approval. With each passing year, he became more cruel behind closed doors. He was abusive in every way you could abuse someone though somehow he managed to restrain his physical abuse. He backhanded me in anger twice, once on the arm, once on the leg. Both times saying, "Relax, it was a joke." He grabbed me and used his size to intimidate me or forcibly push through doors when I tried to remove myself from his raving. He was a bullying, threatening menace. He ridiculed me. He criticized everything I

193

did. The emotional and psychological abuse were the most damaging. He kept everything in the gray and his behavior was hidden from others. The cognitive dissonance was so profound that I couldn't see the abuse until I was in the discard phase, and a therapist helped me understand what I was experiencing. It took months of living alone in silence to get my bearings.

While I was recovering, I learned he had done this to others before me.

It was a short relationship that lasted far too long and cost me nearly everything I had worked towards in my adult life. During the worst of it, I was fading away. I was dying. I didn't want to live. I became a shell of myself. Until you have lived with someone on this spectrum, you cannot understand what it does to your mind. Recovering from this relationship was the hardest thing I have done in my life, and that is saying something. I had only shared the innermost details of this relationship with my therapist. Somehow, Haripriya *knew* and was asking me to go into the dark and face him.

"Tell him you forgive him for trying to destroy you."

I didn't want to forgive him. He didn't deserve my forgiveness. I wasn't his only victim. I wouldn't be his last.

I could feel the knot in my belly was like a tumor and that's when I knew, for certain, I was ready to forgive him, so I could be free of him. My forgiveness was not for him. It was for me.

I forgive you for trying to destroy me.

"Tell him you forgive him for torturing you."

I began to cry. This was much harder than the others. This was the abuser I couldn't talk about. The darkest days of my life.

I— I forgive—I forgive you for torturing me.

Tell him you forgive him for trying to break you.

My breath and crying were more labored, not only because I was reconnecting with the despair I felt during that time in my life, but because no one had ever accurately described or validated my

194

experience and yet, here was an energy healer who knew nothing of my past and somehow, knew everything. I felt understood. I felt compassion for myself.

I forgive you for trying to break me.

"Tell him you forgive him for taking everything from you."

I forgive you for taking everything from me.

It was at that moment that *my* voice showed up, and I forgave him in my own words—*I forgive you for taking my home, property, livelihood, for claiming my ideas and work as yours, for not treating me the way I deserved to be treated. I forgive your lies. I forgive you for harming my relationships. I forgive you for not loving me the way I deserved to be loved. I forgive you for not healing.*

"Can you see him?"

Yes.

"What color is his soul?"

Black, like my Father's.

"Can you send this black soul love and compassion?"

Yes.

She began pushing into my belly again as if she were trying to find something. Then, she paused and said, "Tracie, there is another scene. One that is in a bedroom. Another time you had no voice and no way to fight back. Let's go there."

I knew she was asking me to be present with the night I was raped. I was dating a young man who was a bit older. I was seventeen, and he was nineteen. I was at his house with a small group of friends. He prepared a drink for me and shortly after consuming it, I began to feel dizzy and sedated. The last thing I remember is saying, "I don't feel well. I need to lay down." He guided me to the bedroom, and I passed out on the bed. I understand now that he put a drug in my drink, and I lost consciousness. The next thing I remember was waking up with him on top of me, but I was still in a stupor. He hurriedly got dressed and said, "Don't tell anyone about this." But I knew what happened. The soreness between my legs was a reminder for days. Because I was drugged, I couldn't consent, fight back, or scream.

Haripriya straddled my legs again, and this time she said, "Squeeze my thighs as hard as you can." I was confused for a moment but realized she was creating a "fight back" experience for me.

As I did this, she pushed deep into my belly and I felt a tremendous jolt of pain while she compelled me to, *"Scream!"*

I saw a flash of that scene and screamed, and then I cried. When I finally settled down and stopped, I felt completely empty. The feeling was similar to what I experienced after the dynamic meditation Haripriya instructed. The dynamic meditation seemed to clear energetic blockages in the physical body from stored or unexpressed emotions, and this experience seemed to clear energetic or karmic attachments with others.

I remained on the floor, in the dark, while she placed one hand gently on my forehead saying, "Good girl" in the most sweet, divinely Mothering voice.

The phrase was so simple and so very western, but I had been waiting my whole life to hear it. The Divine was working through her, and I felt its presence.

I can't explain her gifts, and there are probably thousands of academic types that would criticize her method of healing. I would invite anyone with those criticisms to make room for possibility and to acknowledge the outcome she facilitated for me. What happened in that little, dark room with Maa Haripriya was the most potent form of healing I have ever experienced, and I have spent thousands of dollars on therapy and self-improvement. She gave me access to freedom that I have never found through conventional western means. She helped me wipe the slate clean.

Why do we carry these things? Why don't we scream?

After Haripriya excused herself, I stayed in the room alone for a while and used the quiet stillness to integrate. I felt a change in my body and energy. I was so grateful that there was no one to hear my screams; all of the students were gone for the month, and the new residents hadn't arrived.

I made my way down the stairs to the ashram's lobby and was relieved to find it empty. I sat on the sofa by the window with my new feeling of vacancy.

I was startled by the sound of the front door opening, and I turned to see Guru Vishnu entering. I bowed my head, "Guru."

"Hello Tracie. How are you?"

"I've been better."

He tilted his head and paused for a moment asking, "Would you like me to sit?"

"Yes. Please."

He sat beside me and asked, "What is troubling you?"

"Well, I just had a session with Maa Haripriya"

He smiled, "Ahh, I see."

"And, I don't feel ready to go home. I feel like I'm so close to finding the answers I need."

"Now that you have identified the cause of the suffering within you, you must become like a child again: free, joyful, and at ease. You must find the ease within. Stay with us as long as you need. Until you have found this place and you are satisfied."

"I'll think on this. I have to decide soon."

"OK, Tracie. We are here if you need support."

I thanked him for his time and made my way back to the hotel. On the walk, I felt an odd dizziness and emptiness I can't explain. My abdomen felt as though I had just had surgery. Like something was missing. When I reached my room, I showered, curled up in bed and slept until the following morning. After nearly fourteen hours of sleep, I awoke still aching and sore, but I understood the necessity of making those energetic drains in my body conscious.

March 27

Today I had my first class with Master Badoni. I'm studying Pranic healing with him. He demonstrated an energy scan technique on me and immediately started describing my recent relationship. "It looks good from the outside, but you are like a child in a cage. You are not able to be free. You are not able to speak your mind freely. You are not being loved authentically. This is controlling—attachment. This is part cycle. You have to break the cycle in order to thrive in your purpose."

* * *

Master Badoni's assessment seemed to echo the words of Guru Vishnu—*"You must become like a child again. Free, joyful, and at ease."* Like every spiritual teacher I had encountered, He seemed to see my truth as though it were written across my forehead. After an hour of instruction with him, I began to feel a new level of strangeness. It felt like a vortex of disorienting energy was swirling around me.

The feeling of unease had been present since my appointment with Haripriya, and it had intensified. I returned to my room and once again fell into a deep sleep. I had no fever or other signs of illness, just dizziness, disorientation, and the feeling that something in my gut had been surgically removed and was healing.

On the third day, the feeling persisted, and I decided to visit the nearby pharmacy to seek counsel. On the walk there, I felt as though the Earth was off-kilter, or I was. I didn't feel like I was standing upright. I felt askew or tilted. I felt strangely detached, like I was witnessing my body walking and observing everything through my eyes as if through the peephole of a door. The noises of the street sounded far away, like muffled echoes.

What the fuck is happening?

I reached the pharmacy, weak, and fading. I explained my symptoms, and the pharmacist gave me an arsenal of medications to cover every possibility. Antibiotics, antiprotozoal, and hydration salts. I bought them, but intuitively, I suspected I was experiencing some sort of spiritual sickness. A soul level purging.

I returned to my room and stared at the ceiling for hours. Something in what Master Baldoni said evoked an image in my mind. I could see my childhood self with long blond pigtails, feeling sad and alone, in a gilded cage within my heartspace. In a symbolic act of permission, I opened the door to the cage. I reimagined her happy and free within my heart, like a singing bird on a wooden swing. A swing like the one my Grandfather made for me. I saw her joyful; swinging freely and laughing. *Safe.* I committed to keeping her that way.

It was time to manifest a new path forward. It was time to reopen my heart. For good this time. Not just a short-term fix. A long-term, viable, self-respecting, self-loving path forward.

March 30
Today I met with H.N. Kukreti, Narendra's astrologer, and his granddaughter served as translator. Through her, he explained that my chart could answer some of what I was experiencing. My primary planet is Jupiter, the planet of knowledge, prosperity, and good health. "You will be successful in all endeavors. Your Moon is placed in the 4th House in Pisces in Revati Nakshatra, which indicates you are on a journey of spiritual growth and enlightenment. You have psychic abilities and strong mothering instincts. You are in a Moon phase until the full moon in April next year. It is good that you are wearing moonstone over your heart to satisfy your moon. The problems you are experiencing are caused by Ketu who is the tail of the great dragon and it is retrograde in the spiritual or dharma house of your natal chart. He has been causing trouble because he is awakening you and guiding you to your spiritual purpose. He is blocking you from profit

until you step into your role. His persistence will ease by the end of this year. The head of this dragon, Rahu, is in the part of your chart calling you to teach, facilitate, and communicate. You will be successful and financially independent with no debts or enemies." She paused her translation while her grandfather opened a seemingly ancient Sanskrit book with symbols and handwritten notes in the margins. There were as many handwritten paper notes between the pages as actual pages. This was his life's work. He seemed to be searching for something, and then pointed to his discovery. "He says you require a mantra as a remedy to appease Ketu. Chanting this mantra is a sign of devotion to your spiritual journey. You need to repeat this mantra 17,000 times, 108 times after the sun sets starting this Saturday. I can't translate this exactly because it is an ancient beeja mantra, so I will say it and you can write down the sounds. Repeating this mantra will make Ketu happy—settle him down. Ask for his blessings on your spiritual journey."

Om Pram Prim Praum Sah Kate-avay Namaha

* * *

That evening, I was still feeling energetically out of sorts, so I stayed in my room and researched Ketu, the "tail of the dragon" or "shadow planet" that I had never heard of before that day. According to Vedic astrology, Ketu wreaks havoc by creating hard times (check), upset of plans and relationships (check), loss of possessions (check), and creates emotional disturbances like fog, doubt, and confusion (check, check, check) to initiate spiritual awakening or a spiritual quest.

As kooky as this might sound to anyone else, this was an explanation that made sense of my life and experiences, specifically the past two relationships. Each of these relationships was devastating in their own way, but they propelled me further into spirituality. And I rather like the idea that there's a Universal clock in the heavens bringing everything into some kind of Divine cosmic order, placing us in the orbits of others and delivering the lessons that move us forward in our growth and evolution.

After sunset, I chanted the mantra given to me by the astrologer 108 times (plus, one for the Guru). While chanting, I began to connect with the feeling of mercy. With each repetition, I asked the Universe for help clearing karma I have accrued, so I could be free of suffering. *Free.*

As my chanting continued, I felt heavier and heavier, as if I had taken a sedative. It took all of my energy to make it through the entire mala before praying, "Let me be free of this pattern." Then I fell fast asleep.

March 31

It's Easter Sunday and there's really no better day on the calendar to rise from the dead. After chanting the beeja mantra the astrologer gave me. I fell asleep, but woke many times. I was still very sick (even now) and my chest was buzzing with wild energy. I didn't fall into a sound sleep until 4 a.m., and then I had a very powerful dream. In the dream, I was talking to someone at the Cafe—the coffee shop I go to here. I was standing at the counter by the street. I felt pressure on my foot and ankle as if someone were leaning into me. I didn't want to turn to look. I felt the pressure build and push into my outer thigh and hip. I turned to look to my left and there was a very dark-skinned man covered in some kind of oily ash body paint. Whitish-gray in color. He was crouching low, and grunting, and he scared me. I looked to others, but no one intervened. He appeared to be a Sadhu or holy man. He was bent over and looked up at me briefly revealing long eyelashes on his left eye. Only his left eye. Then he continued grunting, which felt like primal chanting because it was guttural. I was afraid of him. Then, I felt a sharp claw sink into my right hand. I felt the points of it make contact. Like a dragon—like a talon. I woke up with a complete memory of the dream and every detail, as if it was real and had happened. The colors. The textures.

I thought about what the astrologer said, and I wonder if my mantra summoned him. Now that he is acknowledged and I have accepted the fear, will I progress? I asked myself what is my intuition around this? What I concluded is, this sickness is a spiritual detoxification. I have purged everything from my gut and through my pores. At the same time I felt ill, my body was buzzing with energy. It's almost as if with every bit of darkness I face, new energy is pouring in to fill the emptiness. Beautiful energy.

I meditated on my future self. What did I see? I saw myself in a garden, near a river, and there were two chairs in the garden. I was sitting in one, and to my right, my partner. I could not see his face, but I knew he was waiting for me in the future. There was a tall tree, like an oak, and my son was there pushing a little girl in a wooden swing—like the one my grandfather had made for me. I could see two mountains in the distance, and a river ran through them. I have not yet seen this place, but somehow, it is a memory to me.

I want that future.

* * *

This was not the first time I went into the darkness of my past, and the spirit world called to me. It was not the first place I met spiritual teachers who painted their bodies with oil and ash. Something about this was reminiscent of my time with the Tsáchila in Ecuador.

Exactly one year earlier, I was staying with the Calazacon family of indigenous Tsáchila healers in the tropical jungle of Santo Domingo de los Colorados. At the time, I was exploring indigenous wisdom around healing, specifically trauma. I was referred to the family by one of my spiritual teachers.

The Tsáchila were a close-knit community of kind and humble people whose healing traditions had been passed down orally since the beginning of time. Their understanding of plant medicine was vast, and their willingness to share that knowledge attracted spiritual seekers from the farthest corners of the world. My experience with them was one of the most profound cultural immersions of my life.

When I arrived on their ancestral land, I met my translator Stephanie, and she escorted me to a bamboo-framed public house with a palm roof where I waited to be introduced to my healer and guide, Juan Calazacon. The moment Juan arrived and sat down across from me, a powerful earthquake began to shake the table, the posts, the roof, and the earth under my feet.

I looked at Stephanie, who was also stunned, and asked, "Is this normal?"

After a quick exchange with Juan, she replied, "He says this is a good sign. Mother Earth is renewing herself." Then she added as an aside, "I've never experienced this here."

The timing of the quake made everything that happened after our meeting feel more profound as if *I needed to pay attention. This was important!* If the earthquake had happened a day before or after, or maybe even an hour before or after, I would not have felt our meeting was so special, but the earthquake happened at the exact moment of our introduction to each other.

Juan exuded peace, and I instantly felt at ease in his presence. His first priority, after welcoming me, was to explain his appearance, which he presumed I would find puzzling. He wore a horizontally striped black and white fabric cloth tightly skirted around his hips. His hair was closely shaven around the sides and back and the longer dark hair on his crown was combed forward to a point. It was perfectly groomed with a thick, red paste derived from the fruit of the Achiote, which inspired the shape and style.

He explained that when the Tsáchila were dying in great numbers from the smallpox epidemic, their Ponés, what we might call Shaman, sat in a three-day Nepi (which is better known to Westerners as Ayahuasca) ceremony, and the plant's spirit told them to paint their bodies with red and black paint to recover from the disease. They extracted the red paste from the annatto fruit, painted their bodies as prescribed in their visions, and indeed recovered. The Tsáchila continued to paint their skin in this sacred manner, garnering the name "Colorados" (meaning "the red-colored ones") by Spanish colonists.

Juan was the picture of health and fitness. His mostly bare skin was painted with unique marks and patterns, with lines circling his calves and arms. A small circular pillow-like object was affixed to the top of his head. He was patient with the translator as she repeated his words in English.

Over the course of a few days, I participated in several ceremonies with Juan and his family. These ceremonies were used to facilitate energetic clearing and cleansing, to heal, and to restore health, which could include inner vision and alignment with the spiritual self.

On the first day, Juan led me on a hike through the jungle to several mountain waterfalls, each higher than the last, while he foraged for medicinal plants along the way. At the highest waterfall, I was instructed to allow the moving water and vapor to cleanse my outer spirit body, focus on my breath, and contemplate on my intentions for the later ceremony in silence.

On the hike back, Juan accommodated all my questions. *What's this? What's that? Is this poisonous?*

I stopped in the jungle for every caterpillar, butterfly, and unusual plant. Stephanie later informed me, "He was observing you during the walk. The jungle told him which plants you need for healing. He said you have a very strong connection with

Mother Earth. He also said your partner's energy is explosive, like a volcano."

True.

The plants Juan collected during our hike were later used in an unusual ceremony, which left me feeling better than I had felt in years. I was asked to sit on a wood bench that stretched across the back edge of a seemingly bottomless pit in the earth about fifteen inches in diameter. The hole was partially filled with water, and there was a length of dried bamboo across the opening where I was to rest my feet. Juan dropped the plants he had collected on our hike into the pit. His brother had gone to the river that morning and intuitively selected a stone for my healing.

Stephanie translated, "He goes to the river and asks the river for your stone. The stone that is yours—one that will not explode in the fire."

My stone was placed in a fire all day until it was white hot, and then it was dropped into the herb-and water-filled hole beneath my feet. On impact, the water boiled and created a massive cloud of fragrant vapor. Blankets were placed over me, creating a makeshift steam bath. I sat under the dark of the blankets, breathing in the botanical steam and sweating buckets for what felt like a century. There were moments I felt as though I would faint, but I toughed it out, only opening my blankets a couple of times for gulps of fresh air.

After the steam ceremony, I was ritualistically bathed. Cold water was mixed with flowers and herbs in a wooden barrel. Then the water was ladled over my entire body. The temperature of the water shocked me awake and alive.

I was given time to rest after these ceremonies, but I felt invigorated. I couldn't rest; I couldn't sleep; and I couldn't eat because I was fasting in preparation for the final Nepi ceremony.

After sunset, I was called to their round hut used for a fire ceremony. In many Spanish-speaking cultures, this structure is referred to as *temāzcalli*, which roughly translates to "house of sweat" in English. The primitive building was partially subterranean and crafted from a guadua (bamboo) frame with a large, round palm roof that hovered about a foot above the earth. An opening in its center allowed smoke to rise and provided a small view of the stars.

Around the central fire pit were two tiered rings that served as both seating and backrests. Juan instructed me to spend time in contemplation with the fire while reflecting on questions I wanted to answer. I sat in the ring alone, and the dancing fire was beautiful to witness. I could hear the sounds of the jungle over the pops and hisses of burning wood. I dropped into a meditative state, feeling a bit nervous about what I was about to do while keeping my mind trained on my intentions for the Nepi ceremony with the Calazacons.

Then, something caught my attention. What appeared to be a snake was moving around the base of the fire. I sat there frozen and watched as a black snake came out of the fire pit and stretched up the edge, holding its head tall. It froze and appeared to be looking at me. I was afraid to move. I managed to squeak out, *"Stephanie,"* calling for my translator, but no one heard me. *"Juan."*

Then the snake did something completely counterintuitive. It returned to the fire. *Why would a snake go into the fire?* I couldn't take my eyes off the flames because I needed to know where the snake was! My nervous system was alert and online. I could no longer think about burning questions or answers for the ceremony because all I could think about was *the snake*.

When Juan and Stephanie returned to collect me for the ceremony, I described what I had just witnessed and expressed my concern (which was more like alarm). An unseen snake was somehow worse than seeing one on the ground in front of me. I knew it was there *but where*?

Stephanie looked at me bewildered; then she looked at the fire, and then she looked back to me again.

"Snakes in this part of Ecuador are venomous."

She had a brief exchange with Juan, who started smiling and nodding his head as if to say, "Ahhh . . . I see." Then he clasped his hands in front of his stomach in a gesture that conveyed that he was pleased, which was thoroughly confusing for me. I was certain something was lost in translation. Stephanie turned back to me and said, "He says don't worry. They don't have snakes."

I appealed, "There is definitely a snake in here. It came out of the fire, looked at me, then went back into the fire."

She translated for Juan, and then she turned back to me.

"He said this snake will not harm you."

I think it's really important to mention I was completely sober at the time this happened.

I was escorted into the subterranean ceremonial space, which was covered by a palm roof. It felt like a womb of clay and was warmed by candlelight emanating from a niche altar with an assortment of objects. I sat on a primitive, wooden bench with my back to the cool earth of the wall while Juan, Manuel, and Twinzaa Calazacon began drumming and singing icaros (sacred medicine songs).

It was a deeply immersive and meditative experience, and the elder, Manual, began cleansing my energy body with rattles and the clacking of stones. When he was satisfied, he served me a smooth seed shell, about the size of a coconut half, filled with liquid. He gestured for me to drink it quickly.

I held the primitive wood cup to my mouth, and at the first taste of the liquid on my lips, I knew the only way I could drink it was if I swallowed it all at once. When I did, I felt it carve a path of fire all the way to my stomach and find its way to every nerve in my body.

The Calazacons continued their loud and immersive singing and drumming. I could see the night sky through a small, circular opening in the central peak of the round roof, and I kept my gaze focused on that for a while until I heard the disembodied voice of a woman say, "She's ready. Let's begin."

The music changed dramatically, and I felt drunk. Or, what I imagine it feels like to be that drunk. I could barely sit up, let alone stand. After thirty minutes of intensifying effects, I asked to return to my hut so I could lie down in my bed. This was apparently not customary, but it's what I wanted so they conferred with each other and then accommodated my request.

I was escorted to my cabin with a trash can in case I began to purge; however, I did not get sick. Instead, I went on an amazing journey to everywhere and nowhere under a canopy of mosquito netting in the Ecuadorian jungle.

I can't define "who" was guiding me on this journey, but Juan later explained that my guide was the plant's spirit.

She showed me how the energy of the Creator, the Universe, is woven through everything; how thoughts and words influence and manifest reality. I experienced oneness and understood that separation is an illusion. I was at once the plants, the person, the medicine, and the frequency of Divine love. I am merely an expression of the creative force alive in every manifestation of this reality like the way a flower appears on a vine or a leaf on a tree. We are all part of a greater unified organism with its own, natural rhythm and cycle.

I was shown that my words are energy carried on sound vibration or waves and the words deliver information as well as my intention. Maybe that intention is to make well, resolve, understand, teach, praise, or a thousand other things, but regardless, to speak a word uses energy to create and send a package to others. This energy must be used wisely.

I was shown what I will create in this world by aligning my intentions and energy with my actions.

This journey lasted all night, and I was shown things I still do not understand, but it was made clear to me that creativity, communication, expression, healing people, and the planet are important parts of my path. The following morning, I met with Juan to integrate my experience. He explained that he was journeying with me and able to view my experience. Stephanie translated. *"Manual, said you have some of the most powerful hands he has ever experienced, and you are meant to heal others. While he was working in your energy field, your hands were creating healing energy. He said you have the gift of sight, and after a near death experience, you can move between the worlds. It is rare that we see an aura like yours. It is very pure. You need to protect your energy from people who will drain you. Most people from the west get sick when they meet Nepi because they need to purge the toxins and drugs in their system. You did not get sick. This is good."*

He continued with folded hands, allowing pauses for translation. "You did not see a real snake in the fire. Mother Nepi came to you in a vision. Mother Nepi takes the form of this snake. She came to you because you are ready to work with her spirit and prepare her medicine. If you would like to come back and stay with us, we will teach you how to prepare her medicine. You are meant to be a healer."

As I reflected on that experience, I realized I have been on the path all along. My energy healing journey began with Shmuel. I was clearing my own energy and learning to heal others with Maa Haripriya. I had experienced my partner's eruption and now understood how that impacted my energy. I needed to acknowledge and heal my relationship pattern to *protect my energy*. One year had passed since that experience, and I was stepping into a new understanding of it.

I had gone into the dark. Into the dirt. I had been unearthing and excavating everything inside of me that needed to be brought to light. I thought these were wounds, but they were actually jewels.

I began to seriously consider staying in India to find the answers I sought. Why not? A month of room, board, and instruction in India was less than a month's rent in the states. The biggest expense, or prohibiting factor, would be airfare, and I doubted that I could reschedule my departing flight economically. I wouldn't be able to stay if it was hundreds of dollars, but I made a deal with the Universe, *If you make it financially feasible, I will take it as a sign that I should stay.*

I went to the river to contemplate and sit in the healing morning sun. On the return walk to the hotel, I passed several chai stalls and cafes in favor of my preferred beverage, Vikas' ginger-lemon-honey tea, which I enjoyed on the balcony.

Narendra joined me and was eager to know if I found answers with his astrologer.

"Thank you. He was so helpful. There are still a few things I need to answer, so I may stay in India a bit longer."

I hadn't told Narendra much about my personal life before that moment, but for some reason, it felt like the right time to share more details. I told him what happened in Ecuador and what I was hoping to solve before returning. I watched emotion cross his face while sharing my experience. Protective anger, empathy, peace.

"No one deserves to be treated that way, especially you. I could see your goodness the moment we met. Women are to be revered. You are the creators of life and deserve better than this." He wrinkled his face and gestured as if he were brushing away rubbish. "Let him go. God is removing this from your life, so you can accept what he has prepared for you. I do not fear losing anything because it was never mine. Everything belongs to God. If God wants me to have money, I will be grateful and do good with it. Everything I have is by the grace of God. God will provide for you."

I spent an hour talking with Narendra in the sun, with a view of the Ganga, and thanked God for his presence and the kismet of our friendship.

When I returned to my room, I called my airline and fully expected a last minute change to be between $700 to $1,200 which meant I was flying home on my existing ticket. The agent said, "Keeping the same itinerary on the same day next month will result in a change fee of one hundred and twenty three dollars."

Seriously? $123.

The decision was as easy as 1-2-3.

I decided to stay in India.

Let There Be Light

My mysterious illness seemed to disappear suddenly as soon as I made the decision to stay in India and once again, I found myself dragging my baggage along the same route between hotel and ashram.

Smiling Manisha was still at the front desk and happy to see me returning. She gave me the key to my room and a new stack of books. This time, I was enrolled in a 300 hour Kundalini course, so I could work more closely with Haripriya and deepen my understanding of this form of yoga while giving myself time to make important decisions.

Most of the arriving faces were new, but there were a few holdouts. For me, that first day was very different from the day I had arrived one month earlier. *I was different.*

In a short period of time, I had healed so much, learned so much, and recognized that I knew very little, if anything at all.

The Kundalini schedule had less free time than the Hatha and Ashtanga curriculum and from the first day, there was a different feel. For starters, my group was small. Thirteen people including me. The classrooms were smaller and warmer with earthen or brick walls and wood floors.

Aside from Haripriya and my alignment teacher Ashutosh Mishra, my instructors were new to me, all male, and there was a theme among them. They were all mysterious and energetically or personally powerful.

In my experience, Kundalini practitioners seemed to have a force field around them more like teachers in a mystery school than a yoga ashram, and within a week, I would confirm that hunch.

Each day, following 5 a.m., Sādhanā with Maa Haripriya, we spent an hour and a half learning pranayama, meditation, and shat kriya (the six cleansing practices) under the tutelage of Yogi Sunil Bisht. I swear when he walked into the room, you could feel the energy change and the temperature drop. He looked like an Indian version of the Scottish actor Gerard Butler, and his eyes smoldered as if there were a faint smudge of kohl around them. Maybe there was. Until meeting him, I had never experienced the type of personal mastery he exuded, and his knowledge of breathwork and meditation was as impressive as his command of the English language. His power was similar to that of my new Kundalini teacher, Yogi Praveen Rajput, who had a mysterious regalness about him, and I perceived him as a psychic wizard of sorts. He would walk through the room and seem to know what we were feeling. Sometimes he paused instruction, narrowed his eyes and asked, "What's going on with you today?" If I was in a deep meditative state with eyes closed, I could feel his energy nearing before I heard his almost silent footsteps. He held a powerful space and amplified the energy in the room.

My new Philosophy teacher, Vishnu Ji, was *always* meticulously dressed in finely tailored clothing and perfectly coiffured. I'd never seen an older gentleman endowed with so much healthy, lustrous hair, and his mustache could make a man of any age envious, I'm sure. He was the wise sage of the lot. I suspected he could see every situation from a 20,000-foot view, and he probably owned a crystal ball.

Hatha instruction continued with Pradeep Aswal, a young master who, at face value, was the most serious and militant of the bunch (or, so I thought) and I had in-depth studies of Ayurveda and Anatomy with Anant Jethuri, who was so divinely enchanting that I could listen to him read a book on the history of computer programming (no offense) without missing a word.

I can't say that I have ever been in an environment in which masculine men were in touch with their feminine intuition and flow. All of the instructors seemed to exist on a different plane, and I wanted to reach it. Making the decision to stay and strive for that lofty goal meant committing to the practices, remaining open to possibility, and surrendering to the process.

216

Kundalini is very different from other types of yoga and is nothing like yoga of the west, which is primarily focused on fitness. It's a spiritual or energetic practice, and the objective is not to perfect the body; it is to clear the mind and energy body so they are receptive to Divine energy allowing higher states of consciousness to be attained. The ultimate goal is *samadhi* or complete absorption with the Divine (bliss). This can be achieved in many ways and one of those paths is through *kriya*, which translates to "effort" or "action." Kundalini is the energy and kriya is the effort or action used to move, manipulate, or harness that energy. Kundalini kriya combines breath (pranayama) with sound (mantra) and movement (asana) to this end. Vishnu Ji described Kundalini as the "Royal Path" or highest form of yoga. My own experience with it was earth shaking.

Literally.

It is recommended that students practice Hatha yoga for two years prior to starting a journey with Kundalini. Hatha balances the energy of the body, specifically masculine and feminine energy, so you are better prepared to handle rising Kundalini or Shakti energy. This energy is said to originate at the base of the spine and rise upward like a serpent through an energy channel called the Sushumna. With time and practice, this feminine energy rises upward to reach the pineal gland, or third eye energy center, where it joins with the energy of the conscious masculine, also referred to as Shiva. The merging of these two energies results in the union of Shiva and Shakti, or masculine and feminine, which purportedly awakens dormant energy channels and expands the capacity of the mind and consciousness. This experience of unification is called a *Kundalini awakening*.

Students were advised against sharing experiences with each other while we were in the program, but we were encouraged to communicate with the teachers. At first I didn't understand this instruction, but having given it thought, I assumed this was to prevent impressioning the mind with what the experience should or shouldn't be and to curtail judgment. In short, whatever the student experienced was exactly the experience they were meant to have.

Kundalini practices are rooted in personal devotion, detachment, withdrawing attention from the outer world and placing it inward or on the subtle body, which is our psychic or energetic experience of this reality. To facilitate an inner experience, there was little time for socializing or cooperative exercises, and silence was imposed from the start of dinner Wednesday until after breakfast Friday morning.

I enjoyed these periods of quiet. I've always been at my best when I can retreat into the rest of silence to restore. When I was young, I intuitively regulated my overly-stressed nervous system by sitting alone in the grass and making flower crowns from clover, walking barefoot on the earth, feeling the wind in my hair, or moving undetected through the quiet of the woods. It was always when I pulled back from the fear and noise of life that I found my calm, regulated, peaceful center. For me, the adage, *silence is golden*, rings true.

My first philosophy teacher in the ashram, Swami Shivabrahmananda, a Hindu monk, explained the animating life force is called *prana* and our body receives this pranic energy through sunlight, earth, water, food, and air. The act of breathing is our primary source of prana while excessive talking results in the greatest loss of our stores. We can fortify our energetic reserves by drinking quality water, consuming foods which are high in prana, such as those in a vegetarian diet, spending time in the sunlight, coming into contact with the earth, and improving the quality of our breath. In theory, we can prevent loss of this energy, or conserve it, by spending more time in silence, which has the added benefit of allowing us access to our inner voice and *true self*. There is purpose in the imposed silence of yoga halls, and sacred spaces or sages who adopt "talk less, listen more" practices. The silence is life-giving.

During our silent periods in the ashram, I fought the urge to speak a "hello" to my classmates and instead, I smiled and nodded. I savored my meals in silence and observed my thoughts. I used the time wisely to study, read, and write.

On the first night of silence, a surge of memories surfaced from my time with the Tsáchila, and I realized what I experienced with them, half a world away, was congruent with what I was learning in India. This reinforced for me the need to be thoughtful with my words. *What energy am I sending to another or creating in this world? What energy am I giving of myself? What am I accepting? What do I want my language to create? What do I want to invest my life force in?*

April 4

Today I had my first experience with Shakti energy. It was both frightening and exhilarating. In my morning Kundalini class, we completed a chakra clearing kriya. During meditation we used the vibration of mantra, visualization, and breathing to focus our attention on each energy center. In several, I had huge involuntary jerks and movements which pretty much freaked me out. I experienced bright, momentary flashes of light. Later, in my Kundalini kriya class with Maa Haripriya, I began to shake involuntarily. I felt scared and self-conscious. I felt fear because I couldn't control what was happening. Then I remembered Maa's words, "Do not resist it; allow the experience." I have never felt that much energy coursing through my body. It was like I was plugged into an outlet. It persisted, so I went to my room after class instead of having lunch and waited for the feeling to subside. It lasted an hour. I also had a lot of emotions come up—around André, home, plans— all of it. Everything I am willing to release.

The first experience with Kundalini energy rocked my world. Mostly because I couldn't control it, I could only accept, witness, and allow it. After the experience, my new mission was not to recreate it but to become a non-resistant vessel for the energy. Nothing really prepared me for the work necessary to do that. My experiences continued though some were more subtle than others. I began to sense that I am as much energy as flesh and bone. My life experiences were beginning to come into focus through this lens too including everything I had learned on my spiritual journey thus far, from reiki and pranic healers, shamanic practitioners, spiritualists, indigenous healers, my time in the Light during my near-death experience, and my experience with plant medicine. One thread ran through them—Everything *was energy*. There were no borders, boundaries, and edges between things. We perceive people, animals, nature, objects as separate solids because that is what is necessary for us to navigate the experience of the Earth School. Seeing through the illusion of separateness is the pinnacle of every spiritual journey.

Science shows us that at an atomic level, there is no separation. It is more like the "oneness" so many spiritual thought leaders describe, including Albert Einstein. Going a step further, I believe this is how we will come to understand psychic phenomenon. Brain activity and thoughts are energy too, and it seems silly to believe that energy is confined to the perceived gray matter borders of the human brain. I have had so many experiences with the unexplained or paranormal, and my search for answers reveals an emerging framework to help me better understand them. *Energy.*

April 6
I am having incredible experiences with Kundalini. Today, during kriya, I began to have some electrical sensations, and while

implementing Bhairava mudra, I felt as if really warm, almost hot, honey was moving through and over my hands. It was a strong sensation, the strongest I have ever felt in energy work.

* * *

The following morning, on the first Sunday of the month, I joined a group outing to Vashishta Gufa, the meditation caves Mana said I should visit. The cave complex is about twenty-five kilometers outside of Rishikesh, situated along a peaceful stretch of the Ganga river that runs through rural and agricultural lands. The setting there feels even more sacred because, except for the temple complex, the shores are relatively untouched by human development or commerce.

April 7
Today I joined a group trip to Vashishta Gufa on the banks of the Ganga. I visited two of the primary caves, but I didn't feel anything special. I felt conscious of the fact that others were waiting for access, so I followed an intuitive pull down to the rocky shore then another down the banks of the river. I walked a good distance and thought of Mana's hunch, "I feel you will find something there."

It is said that Jesus meditated here during his missing years. Rishikesh natives repeat this as if it is a known fact and no big deal. There's even a book on the subject. I walked further down the beach to the isolated end, where shore terminates into rock. When I stood there and surveyed the scene I thought, "This is what I want in my life. The sound of water, birds, beauty, mountains. I want to live in a place like this."

I heard a rustling sound behind me and turned to see another cave! I walked over to it and went inside the small opening. Inside, I felt a presence I cannot explain. In my body it felt like pressure. I heard what sounded like murmuring voices coming from within the stone wall in front of me, and then a very loud sound like a slamming door startled me. But it was a cave, and it wasn't anywhere near a house or people. The experience frightened me. It seemed I was unwelcome in someone's home. I went back out into the sunlight and noticed a woman standing on the beach where I had been moments before. She asked, "Did you feel pulled over here too?"

"Yes," I said, then pointed to the cave behind us and told her I would be interested in her experiences there. (I later learned she was a psychic from New Zealand.)

I found a quiet spot on the beach to sit in reflection on the question, "Am I on the right path?" Looking at the green mountains, rocks, and clean rushing water, the only answer I seemed to have was the type of place my soul wanted to live, and I let myself imagine that home in the future. When I started back towards the temple, a miniscule glint in the sunlight caught my attention. It was like the sparkle of a tiny diamond among the vast expanse of rocks that stretched as far as the eye could see. I walked to the spot and bent down to find a tiny sterling silver butterfly charm, about the diameter of a pencil eraser, sitting perfectly atop a stone. The odds of anyone seeing this seemed slim in this landscape.

* * *

Well, Mana was correct. I had found something at the meditation caves. Perhaps that butterfly charm was a little message from the Universe that everything behind me was a necessary part of my evolution and transformation.

Over the weeks that followed, I settled into a deep state of devotion. And in all of the ways my first month in Rishikesh was about examining my ideas around masculine power and energy; the second month was about witnessing feminine power and the Divine feminine. I was surrounded by deep thinking, feeling, and embodied women like two southern California wildcats, an Indian sharp-as-a-tack intellectual, a European psychotherapist, a hilarious writer from New York, a free-spirited young woman from everywhere, an introspective observer from Poland, and the Italian attorney who was so honest about her own journey and in touch with her own needs and desires that I considered her a bonus teacher in the program. I learned so much from these women. The environment they co-created was, in a word, *nourishing*.

April 10
Yesterday was the eclipse and the first day of Navaratri, a nine-day celebration of the divine feminine goddess Maa Durga. Each day is devoted to one of her nine forms.

Kundalini kriya has been bringing up so much energy—yesterday all I could feel was anger. I felt angry about my experience with masculine violence and abuse. But I didn't feel bad about feeling angry, which was new for me. It felt like righteous anger.

* * *

Each day during Navaratri we celebrated in the ashram with Prasad, flowers, dancing, chanting, and lighting oil lamps in the presence of a statue of Maa Durga. After the ceremony the first evening, I sat with Haripriya for a while and shared my experience with André, but of course, she was already aware. I imagine she saw this in my healing session too. She responded so succinctly, "It's not love if it's hurting you."

I felt better having told her myself and saying it out loud. I confessed it was the complexity of the situation that I struggled with. I wondered if my spiritual path as a healer meant that I should remain committed to André. If his diagnosis was cancer I would not have left him.

She asked if I wanted to continue to have the same experience over and over again with a partner that wouldn't do the work to address the violence and womanizing in his life. "It takes conscious choice for someone to heal. They have to choose it."

She explained that now that I am conscious of the pattern, if I return to it, I am responsible for the karma of choosing self-harm.

"I don't want that pattern in my life anymore. I want to be free to express myself. Free to choose. Free to feel my feelings—like anger or sadness."

"Well, then, you know what you want. You have to make a plan, a plan to create a life of peace, love, and safety for yourself."

I was surrounded by unbelievably strong and soft women during a festival that celebrated every aspect of a woman as divine. I guess that gave me the strength I needed to make my appeal to the Universe.

I am ready to create a life of peace, love, and safety. Show me the way.

Not thirty minutes after that prayer, I decided to begin a search for a temporary living situation. When I opened my computer, the *very first* thing I saw was an ad from one of the teachers at the little yoga studio I attended in the mountains. She was looking for a *roommate*. I could not believe it. I sent her a message and within twenty four hours had signed a six-month lease on faith, sight unseen. Two hours after I signed the lease, an acquaintance reached out to me with an unexpected, fully remote job opportunity, and I didn't even have to think about it.

Yes.

I told the Universe I was ready and the steps appeared. I had two of the answers I needed. I had a place to move to as soon as I returned to the states and a new remote job that would allow me to work flexibly while I figured things out.

Just as I was getting ready to inform André of my plans to move, I received a message from him letting me know I had seven days to move out when I returned.

Seven days.

I told him I thought that was unrealistic, especially since I would be returning jet lagged after forty hours of travel. But then I switched gears, and thanked the Universe for letting me see him clearly, providing solutions, and making my decisions so much easier. I didn't know how I was going to make it happen—return home, re-integrate, round up boxes, pack all of my belongings and move out in seven days, but I heard Zoya's voice once more. "If there's anyone who can do this, it's you."

Everything will work out as it should.

My sole purpose had become devotion to the process and allowing the path to unfold.

Trust.

On the fifth day of Navaratri, Maa Haripriya invited students on a trek to Gurdwara Sri Hemkund Sahib, a Sikh temple on the opposite shore in Tapovan. Getting there required a long walk in the heat, a bridge crossing, and a Tuk-Tuk ride through the chaos of the market district.

We arrived at the gates, washed our hands and feet and covered our heads before entering. The exterior of the gilded, white temple was almost modest compared to its grand chandelier-adorned interior with seemingly enough space for 2,000 people. On that occasion it was mostly empty except for our small group and a handful of others sitting with reverence.

As I sat in meditation in that devotional space, I touched into that beautiful deep, calm, nothingness; then I had an unexpected vision that was like a dream. I felt a sacred female presence as if I were in the temple of the Holy Mother. My eyes were closed, but I sensed her approaching me. For some reason, I was fearful of her judgment and couldn't open my eyes to look at her. I felt her circling, examining me, weighing my life, my choices, actions and deeds. She came close to my left ear and asked if I felt I had a good heart. "No. I feel angry at times."

And she replied, "Why should you not feel anger? How you are treated, I am treated."

We are all part of the sacred whole.

I shared most of the walk back with Haripriya but didn't mention my experience in the temple. Instead, I peppered her with questions about her life and journey. Later that evening, I reflected on the day and realized so much of the work I was doing on this trip was around releasing suppressed emotion and energy. My experiences with dynamic meditation, energetic healing, and Kundalini were all clearing traumatic moments in my life when my voice was silenced, and I was unable to fight back, or express my feelings. It was completely appropriate to feel angry with André. It was appropriate to feel betrayed. I was going to let myself feel it, so I could heal it.

The experience in the temple reminded me of a passage I had once read in which Saint Hildegard described her vision of Mother Mary. "She is so bright and glorious that you cannot look at her face or her garments for the splendor with which she shines for she is terrible with the terror of the avenging lightning, and gentle with the goodness of the bright sun; and both her terror and her gentleness are incomprehensible to humans . . . But she is with everyone and in everyone, and so beautiful is her secret that no person can know the sweetness with which she sustains people and spares them in inscrutable mercy."

I suppose that kind of pure, unconditional love is terrifying because it is so powerful that it can destroy any illusion. In that way, love is destructive in the same way as truth and consciousness are destructive.

April 14
I've been clearing old energy in my daily kriya practice each day, with each chakra. For the first two chakras, Muladhara and Svadhistana, I felt fear and sick with digestive upset. In the third

chakra, Manipura, I felt heat, empowerment, and began sweating. In the heart chakra, Anahata, I felt a lot of emotional upset—anger, anxiety—energy in and around the heart, and lots of it. I had been trying to access my intuition, but I think I was a little too distressed. Yesterday during the Anahata kriya, I felt a release, then had a vision of my future, my life in a complete download. I saw everything come together as it was always meant to. Everything I lost was only making room for what is to be. I felt grateful. I heard this message clearly, "There are three ways to realize your desires: work for them, manifest them, or allow them." Hearing this made me realize there are ways I don't allow myself to have what I want. So, I'm giving myself permission to have it all.

* * *

I made a return trip to Kunjapuri temple for the mountain sunrise, but this time, I only felt wonder and joy. I had come so far since my last visit.

So far.

I returned to Rishikesh and joined Mana for Prasad. Instead of fruit or rice, she prepared a large vat of rose milk and ladled it into cups for those passing by her door. The beverage was the same color as the strawberry milk I drank as a young girl, but it was flavored with rose. I don't normally drink milk, but it was an indulgent treat, like a milkshake. It was hot that day, so people were especially grateful for cold refreshment, and it wasn't long before the last of it was served.

Mana and I retreated to the cool shade of her studio floor and settled onto cushions and commenced our girl talk. Our conversation steered to something so few in my inner circle can relate to: Having the "gift" of *sight*.

Mana shared her experience with intuition, visions, and her own Kundalini awakening. Then, she asked, "When did you first realize you were psychic?"

Mana, like every spiritual teacher or mentor I had met, knew I had this "gift," but it was a part of myself that I kept secretive or filed away because as a child, I just wanted to be "normal" (whatever that is). Sharing this part of my life was much more challenging than divulging details about personal relationship failures, experiencing loss, or recovering from trauma and abuse. The reason is that those are things that happened to me. Having the "gift," or psychic abilities, is who *I am*. And so, sharing this requires vulnerability and trust. Mana, I trusted. She could understand me in ways most people could not and so, I started at the beginning.

"Around age six, I saw an apparition that I would later understand was my first spirit guide, a Native American man given the name Joseph by Catholic missionaries. From that moment on, I began to see energetic remnants of buildings that no longer stood; I had visions, saw the departed, and I knew things I had no business knowing. I remember one morning at the breakfast table, my Mom started a sentence saying, "I had the weirdest dream last night" and I blurted out what her dream was about because I could see her nightmare as clearly as she had. So my Mom *knew*. She didn't do anything to harm my abilities. She never said, "There's no Indian" or "You can't possibly know that." She believed me, and I think that's why my abilities remained."

Mana nodded, seemingly in agreement.

"Because we lived in a very Christian community and were ourselves Christian, we just had an agreement that we wouldn't talk about it outside of our home. This was for my protection, I guess. I think that's when I subconsciously registered it's not normal to have these abilities and, in order for me to be normal or accepted, safe even, this part of me needed to be a secret.

"Later, around age ten, I had a terrifying experience with a spirit and shut down my sight for years. My abilities returned around age eighteen, but I didn't have mastery over them. It was generally random, like seeing residual energy of people and places, or getting information through one of the clairs—clairvoyance, clairaudience, clairsentience, claircognizance.

"My abilities began to strengthen around the time I conceived my son and intensified after my near death experience, but it was years later—after a devastating relationship with a narcissist brought me to my *dark night of the soul,* that everything came rushing back and was powerfully clear. That's when I recognized my mediumship abilities and when I realized that the communication with the Divine, guides, and guardians goes both ways.

"My experiences with nature and animals during that time led me to mentors that helped me understand what I was experiencing. A shamanic healer walked me through the terrifying experience with the spirit when I was ten. I began to hone my abilities, to understand them as an adult, and to figure out how to work with symbolism. I began to accept and normalize this part of my life as much as I could normalize this part of my life.

"I came to the conclusion that I am merely a channel for information, and I recognized the importance of keeping my energy and vessel clean and so, yoga and meditation were important tools."

It was easy to have a conversation about this with Mana because she understood *sight.*

"What does mediumship look like?," Mana asked.

"Well, I'll give you an example of a time that I was really being pushed to give information to someone, and I didn't want to out myself. I had been spending time with a new friend. One day we were hiking, and I was really enjoying our conversation when an elderly woman appeared to her right. The woman, in spirit form, was persistent in wanting to give my friend a message. I was super afraid to say to this person, *hey, I have a psychic message for you,* but I knew I was being asked by one of her guides to be of service. At the first opening I asked her 'how do you feel about mediumship?' She said, 'you mean, like psychics?' When I realized she was OK with it, I asked her if she was open to receiving information from her guide.

"Something happens when I ask permission, and there is consent. It's like an extension cord between me and the person's guide connects, and information flows so fast I describe it as a *quickening*. I speak rapidly to say everything as fast as I hear it.

"I told her exactly what I saw and heard—*There is an older woman here who appears to be wearing a simple flower print dress from the 1940s. She has gray hair in a bun with round glasses. I'm hearing the name Franny and she says she is your Grandmother. She says you need to make changes with how you deal with the stress in your life. She says you need to start baking, which will teach you to cope with mistakes and recognize your self-speak. She is with you and will support you through this time. You can speak to her.*

"When I finished, my new friend looked at me and said something that made me feel like a fool.

"'I don't have a Grandmother named Franny. But I do need to make changes in my life.'"

"For days I questioned if I should speak up and worried that I had harmed my new relationship with this person. But then, something miraculous happened. Four days later, she sent me a text late at night and said, "'Can I call you?'" When she called she was excited and said, "You're not going to believe this. My daughter has been researching our family tree, and I have a Grandmother named Francis that I never met. Her nickname was Franny. We found newspaper articles that referenced my Grandmother as an award winning baker and guess what? There's a picture. She looks exactly as you described."

"Franny came through for both of us that day and my friend has turned into quite the baker."

Mana was blunt in her assessment, "Why are you afraid of using these gifts?"

"Judgment," I said.

"Well, your work is to recognize this fear of judgment or negative comments and do it anyway."

I said, "It's still random. I don't see a guide with every person I meet. Sometimes I just know what I am meant to pass along. I cannot yet connect or channel on demand, but perhaps that will come in time. When I do get information, I pass it along without judging it. Even if it's just a symbol that might mean nothing to me, like a bagel or a lemon. Sometimes messages are nothing more than sweet connections like a greeting from the other side, and sometimes, they are really hard, and I experience heavy feelings, maybe even the physical sensations of the departed's death. But all of this is used to provide confirmation and relieve fear. Ultimately, it helps people connect to the energy of life and affirms life after death."

In saying all of this out loud to Mana, I recognized the sacredness of the gift I had been given. It made perfect sense that I ended up in an ashram with a Kundalini program, met Raju Baba, and ended up in her company. I had followed all of the steps as they unfolded. Perfectly, as it were.

Mana shared her own initial fears around stepping out of her interior, closely-held world and living large. Then, she paused and looked at me with the softest expression, "Tracie, you can remove all doubts now. André cannot meet you where you are. You are right to release him and make room for the love you deserve. You think the relationship with him was the opportunity of a lifetime, but you can have all of the things you loved about him and so much more."

She was delivering a message to me. It was the one I didn't believe when I heard it myself. She helped me see the value of self-acceptance and authenticity in the space of spirituality. Denying this part of me was no longer an option. My abilities were as natural as my eye color.

I was so grateful for Mana's appearance in my life; for Raju Baba's intuitive connection, and for all of the people who showed up along the way and delivered me to the feeling of wholeness I felt in that moment. This was, in many ways, my shadow. And I had spent the past five years letting this part of my life come to the light.

I can't help but wonder, on a larger scale, how many of us walk around with rejected intuition and abilities because somewhere, along the way, we were told, "there's no one there" or "that's not possible," and instead of trusting ourselves, we conform so we aren't labeled as crazy or ostracized from our communities. What would this place be like if we were free of our fear of death and opened up to the magic? What could we create together?

One of the things travel and cultural immersion taught me is indigenous cultures have preserved knowledge of our inner "extra sensory perception" system. This communication system reaches beyond the physical senses and works with all living things, not just humans. The *Oneness* is waiting for us to come home to the river of life.

Something else I have learned along the way is that the greatest block to our inherited Universal navigational system is fear. We have plenty of that in the "civilized" world, and maybe that's by design. We are more subservient and compliant when we are afraid. We are better consumers when we are less connected to the wisdom of our hearts. As I have learned from my time in the Light, and from every mentor, teacher, and messenger along my path, *fear blocks the heart, and the heart knows the way.*

Sitting with Mana and sharing my secret life so freely made me realize the power of connecting with people who can accept my wholeness without judgment. From my own experience on this journey, I can say with confidence that when we focus our love inward and commit to healing and growth, the Universe aligns us with the people we need along the way. Sometimes, we are meant to walk alone. Sometimes aloneness is the lesson and the catalyst for reconnecting with our true, spiritual nature.

Mana helped me understand another force at work in my new practice. Sexual energy.

The more I allowed my feelings to flow freely in daily kriya, the more my sexual energy amplified. I felt sexually attracted to men in a new way. Energetically. If the man was healed and in flow, I could sense it, and my energetic system responded. When this happened, I would suppress it, which is the equivalent of rejecting it, but it grew stronger.

I shared my recent experience in a class, "The instructor was providing an alignment, and I felt my whole body light up like a Christmas tree when he touched my shoulder."

Mana explained, "This is good. Your sexual energy is rising because you are celibate and performing kriya. Tantra teaches us to harness that sexual energy for creation. Use this energy to give birth to your book!"

My body was disappointed to hear this solution, but my heart and mind agreed that harnessing the energy into a creative project was probably the better channel. What a concept: Put my desire into action instead of denying or suppressing it.

I joked, "From now to the end of the year, the temple is closed for cleaning."

Well, I was only half joking.

The conversation with Mana gave me a new perspective that I took into my daily practice, and instead of suppressing sexual energy when it arose, I began to get curious about it and channel it.

April 20

On the ninth and final day of Navaratri, we celebrated the aspect of the goddess Durga that bestows spiritual knowledge and divine powers. After our devotional practice, the statue which spent nine days as a focal point in our hall, a representation of the Divine feminine within, was carried to the river by Maa Haripriya while we followed in a parade. This was no small task. It was supremely hot, and the statue seemed as big as Maa. I could tell she was giving this mind-over-matter effort with pride and was fueled by the belief she could do it. She carried that statue over a half mile in bare feet. Haripriya's example made me aware of the lack of devotion in my own life.

* * *

On the ninth and final day of Navaratri, out of the blue, I received notice of a $200 cash transfer from an old friend. He was repaying me for something I had long forgotten about and, frankly, had written off. *Thanks Universe!*

With that surprise money, I decided to make self-care my personal devotion to the Divine for the nine days I had remaining. I would care for myself as though *I am* a sacred temple. I have never equated self-care with healthcare. I had always put the needs of others before my own and thought of self-care experiences as indulgent or selfish.

I was so wrong.

When I arrived at this realization, I had the great luck of being in India. India—where self-care *is* healthcare, and nearly every self-care practice is ten dollars. You want a one hour massage? Ten dollars. Need to consult with a doctor? Ten dollars. Psychotherapy? Ten dollars. Reiki? Ten dollars. So with nine days remaining, I decided to spend ten dollars each day on my wellness. I decided to devote ninety dollars to "temple cleaning, repairs, and maintenance."

Each day, during my afternoon break, I had a devotional appointment. First, a consultation with an Ayurvedic doctor who counseled me on eating the right foods for my dosha. Then, a relaxing experience called *shirodhara* which involves pouring a gentle, continuous stream of warm oil over the third eye in the brow center followed by a steam bath. On the third day, I had a massage appointment with a woman so tiny I felt like a giant. But, as they say, never judge a book by its cover. She was small but mighty and at several points climbed onto the table to apply pressure. I was so relaxed afterwards, I could barely move.

April 21

If I had to pick one word to describe today, it would be nourishing. This morning, a few of my classmates and I crossed the Ganga by boat to visit the Tapovan side. We had brunch in a beautiful plant-filled cafe overlooking the Ganga. It was an all-girl crew, and we talked candidly about our female experiences with relationships, motherhood, break-ups, and intimacy. Many of them, farther along on the journey, shared their experience navigating deep transformation. I was grateful for their openness at a time when I'm developing a new understanding of energy and relationship. On the return trip, I noticed over a dozen monkeys in the tree opposite my usual cafe. I hadn't seen them gather like this, and on closer inspection, I realized every one of them had a baby. The image of it—this tree of life—felt synchronous.

After brunch, I joined Mana for tea and sisterhood. We continued our deep conversations about intuition, stepping into visibility, allowing the spiritual path to unfold instead of avoiding it, and past lives. All the while, as we shared this space, she was pregnant with her second child. I felt regret that I wouldn't be there to meet the baby when she arrived.

All day I was surrounded by Divine feminine energy. As I tended to my own, I saw it in others.

* * *

Throughout my bonus second month in India, I was healing my feminine alongside others on a similar path and receiving their support in reclaiming what I had suppressed—my voice, expression, creativity, intuition, and desire.

I had arrived at the final full week of programming, and the new life waiting for me was starting to take shape. I would return to the states with a new way of being in the world—a fresh start on so many levels.

April 22

This morning, I went to 5 a.m. Sādhanā which was normally led by Haripriya. Today, only a dozen people showed up, and we were surprised to find Guru Vishnu in her place. He organized us into a circle and then sat between me and the person to my left. He guided us through a beautiful meditation practice incorporating Nadi bhramari, which I think translates to breathing bee or bee's breath. His meditation was very similar to Tonglen, if it were a Kundalini kriya. Instead of just breathing in suffering and exhaling peace, as with Tonglen, the hands are extended outward in a sweeping, giving gesture with the exhale while holding an intention of sending loving energy to the world. I truly felt my energy was amplified by sitting next to him. I don't think it was an accident that I was having this experience. I think the Universe was giving me the chance to recognize how energy can be magnified when you are surrounded by people aligned with your own energy or intentions. I want to send peace to the world.

After class, Guru Vishnu had the biggest grin; he put his hand on my shoulder and asked, "How are you Tracie?"

He knew the answer to his question. That's why he was pleased.

I am at peace.

Not long after my experience with Guru Vishnu in Sādhanā, I discovered one of the young female residents in the hallway; she was sobbing and in excruciating pain. I sat with her on the floor and immediately had an intuitive feeling that something had ruptured in her pelvic area. Two weeks prior, I was seated near her in class and received a similar intuitive message indicating she had an ovarian cyst. I got the information in a brief flash and didn't say anything because, for all the reasons I have shared, I thought it would seem crazy to tell someone, out of the blue, "Hey, you should have your ovaries examined." I even considered that I was projecting my own medical history onto the young woman. So I ignored my intuition. I said nothing.

While she suffered in pain and awaited transport to the hospital, I stayed with her, holding her hand. She sent me a text later and confirmed there had been a cyst on her ovary. *"Tracie, thank you so much for being with me at this time, for keeping my hand and help! I am grateful, sending love straight from my heart."*

This was a lesson meant for me too. What if I had spoken up two weeks earlier? Could those timely words have prevented her suffering? If the cost of sharing intuitive information was potential ridicule or judgment, the benefits—reducing suffering or worse— far outweighed the risks.

My intuition was back online, and this time I planned to protect it. Returning to a pattern of fear and uncertainty, born from my wounding and self-rejection was not an option. I had cleared the debris that was blocking this channel, like removing mud from a windshield.

To this end, my nine days of daily self-care continued, and I accepted every request to be a subject for those in healing courses. I was an immediate "yes" to anyone who asked, "Do you want to be my practice dummy for . . ." *Yes. Absolutely yes.* Every night I was a practice patient for sound healing classes and energy healing students.

A student from one of these classes introduced me to her teacher, Ankur, and I was so fascinated by his methods that I scheduled an appointment with him as part of my nine-day devotion.

My first session with him was a traditional energy healing session, and afterwards he recommended a therapy that opens up finer physical energy channels in the body.

I returned the following afternoon for my first experience with Marma Point therapy, an ancient healing system similar to acupressure. During a session, the practitioner places pressure on specific points along meridians in the body to improve energy flow.

"Before we began," Ankur explained, "There will be moments that may feel painful. When this happens, say *Hari Om*."

Hari Om is a mantra that is said to remove suffering and blockages of energy in the body. I thought Ankur was giving me a "safe word" of sorts. Like, *when it's too much, say Hari Om, and I'll stop.*

I have a high pain tolerance. Well, I thought I did. But there were incredibly painful points, and one spot on my hand was so intense that I couldn't bear it and gasped *"Hari Om!"* but instead of backing off, Ankur applied even more pressure and when I held my breath and stiffened he said, "Chant Hari Om to activate your inner healer!"

The excruciating pain was the result of a sweet, mild-mannered person applying pressure with one finger to a single point on my hand, and yet the sensation was so intense it rivaled the "ring of fire" phase of giving birth. In a desperate plea to end the sensation, I rattled off enough Hari Oms to rival the Litany of Saints. Then, something transcendent happened.

I felt as though I was in a trance, and I noticed Ankur was singing. *How long had he been singing?* Then I felt something I can't explain. It was as if his energy had merged with mine. I was experiencing some kind of connection with or through him—with masculine energy. Safe, healing masculine energy. It was what masculine energy should feel like. I felt subtle vibrations throughout my body, similar to what I experienced in Kundalini, but this was balancing. I began to observe the pain radiating from the pressure point and, this is going to sound bonkers—it was as though my body was a vehicle; the pain was a diagnostic code providing feedback, and Ankur was a masterful technician providing a tune-up. My guides appeared around me, and this simple healing session turned into one of the most sacred experiences of my life.

Nothing in Rishikesh is ordinary.

That evening, our Hatha instruction was provided on the bank of the Ganga just before sunset during the *golden hour.* The hot Indian sun painted the sky a warm, hazy orange that melted into the green of the mountains and the turquoise of the river while I fell *in love.* I was radiating love and gratitude for my life, my experiences, people, creation—everything. I felt free. I felt strong. I felt whole. In that moment, the Light didn't only exist on the other side of death's door. I could see it was always shining through from the other side. *Everything is illuminated.*

April 25

Today we explored yoga nidra, the psychic sleep, in our meditation class followed by Ajna opening Kundalini kriya. It was a powerful combination, and I'm not sure what I experienced. I'm still processing, but I want to write down the details while it's fresh. When I transitioned from asan to sukhasana for meditation, I began to see (in my mind's eye) an ashy pit with a broken egg in my root-sacral wombspace. With each inhale, I saw energy like a white light snake rising up my central channel. When it reached my thoracic, I saw it spread through every nerve of my body, and I felt a moment of deep,

239

unconditional love in my heart. I began quivering before this—or shaking—and felt I was resisting the rise. I reminded myself to let it happen. Then, I felt and saw it rise higher, coiling into the space of my third eye/Ajna. There was a tremendous amount of light, and rather than something explosive or painful, I felt the safety of masculine energy holding space for the feminine. The shaking continued—involuntarily—and I was overwhelmed with emotion; tears streamed down my cheeks. I stayed there in knowingness and peace for the remainder, seeing this coil of light in my forehead, not wanting it to end.

* * *

My experience with Kundalini, which used breath, movement, and mantra to expand consciousness, was not unlike my experience in the Ecuadorian jungle with the plant medicine of the Tsáchila. Both cultures, separated by thousands of miles, hold sacred the path to oneness by means of a spiritual, energetic snake, a female awakener. And with that, I had a completely new context for the Biblical story of Adam and Eve.

Everything is Energy. Everything is Light.

The End is the Beginning

Raju Baba was traveling to Delhi to see his family, so we had one last talk on his bench under the flowering tree before his departure. He took my hand in his and said, "Obama, I miss you." And when my eyes began to fill with tears he shook his head and said, "No crying over boys!" Then he threw his head back and laughed, pleased with his joke.

What luck I had to be on the road just behind this wacky man who showed me another path, a more suitable path.

Maa Haripriya departed soon after for a holiday in London, and her absence was felt immediately in the ashram.

Though a handful of instruction days remained, the thirteen of us enrolled in the 300-hour program were included in the closing ceremony and graduation of departing students in the shorter programs. That morning, my cohort received our exam results so we could graduate with the group.

Once more, I sat in the hall with a strand of marigolds around my neck. But this time, I would successfully complete 500 hours of instruction and I had the answers I had prayed for. I felt proud of myself. I had mustered the courage to go forward, alone, and worked through deep pain, facing the lifetime of traumas dormant in my nervous system.

To close the ceremony, Guru Vishnu gave an inspiring talk and then asked if any students wished to come to the microphone and share their experience. Many came forward to express their gratitude for what they learned or the connections they made, but I was not one of them. I shrank like a wallflower. Once it seemed there were no other takers, Guru asked, "Is there anyone else who would like to speak?" *Not me.* Then he held an outstretched, inviting palm in my direction and dipped his head a bit, as if to say: *Tracie, this is your moment.*

Surely he wasn't looking at me. I turned my head and looked around me. *Is he talking to me?*

Then, I turned back to him. *He was making eye contact with me.*

"Is there anyone else who would like to speak?"

He was definitely talking to me, and he was waiting for me to accept his invitation. I pointed to myself in a gesture of *Do you mean me?* He, smiled and gave one affirming nod.

Fuck. How can I refuse?

Inside of a pause that seemed like an hour, I felt my heart drop into my stomach; my face flushed; my temperature warmed, and my hands started to tremble, but also, I knew what was happening.

This is my final exam. No plan. No idea what I will say. Will I shrink, afraid to be seen?

I stood with wobbling knees, walked to the front of the hall, took the microphone, and faced the dozens of students staring at me. I don't know what happened, but I surrendered, and the words flowed out of me.

"I didn't come here to be a teacher. I wanted to know myself better. To deepen my practice.

"Just after I planned this trip to India, my entire life fell apart. My relationship, home, and work plans crumbled.

"Originally, I was enrolled at a different school, but when I saw, "Samadhi Ashram" I intuitively thought, *That's what I want.* So, I changed schools at the last minute and ended up here.

"If your life is going to fall apart, I can't think of a better place to rebuild it. To rebuild yourself. I have been nourished by the special people around me, the teachers who are so enthusiastic for their subjects they made me excited to learn. Thank you Guru Vishnu for creating this special place that has felt like home to me.

"I have been so fortunate to be surrounded by all of you during this time— now forever friends. I love you. Thank you for being part of my journey."

I returned to my seat and realized what a gift Guru Vishnu had just given me. In a way, I had provided the closing remarks for our ceremony and for my two months there. I did what I was afraid to do—used my voice to speak what was on my heart, which was the surest sign that I'd reaped results from my time there.

Afterwards, a classmate approached me to share that she was in a similar situation in life and was grateful for my perspective. We hugged, and I regretted I did not know this sooner. Then an Indian mother and daughter pair approached me, and the younger said, "My Mother and I really loved what you shared today. She says you have the smile of an angel." And that made me feel so warm that my eyes filled with tears. How could she think that? I felt compelled to hug them both, so I did.

These were never the outcomes I imagined.

After the ceremony, students bid farewell to each other and began their departures. Within twenty-four hours, only thirteen of us remained.

I received a text message from Haripriya: "Wishing you peace and happiness on your journey always. May you shine your light so others will see theirs and follow your heart. It's time to unclip those wings."

Then I suspected she was the one behind Guru's nudge.

With our small group remaining, the ashram was unusually quiet. I passed no one during my climbs and descents on the stairs. This made our little group even tighter, and I spent many afternoons and evenings at the juice bar around the corner in deep discussions with them.

I had brutally honest conversations about intimate relationships with Francesca, the beautiful (in every sense) and self-aware Italian attorney. I had deep conversations about everything from philosophy to plant medicine with Charley, a personal trainer and sailor from New Zealand. He was exactly as you might imagine a personal trainer and sailor from New Zealand. Part philosophical surfer with long sun-streaked curls that met his shoulders, and part *man of the world* always dressed in a breezy, barely buttoned cotton or linen oxford shirt with sleeves casually rolled. He was rugged and refined. Intellectual and relaxed.

The quiet of the ashram during this period also allowed for more interactions with Guru Vishnu, who wasn't perpetually occupied with classes and students. The morning after the majority of graduates departed, I ran into him in the lobby. He was noticeably happy; his face was bright.

"How are you, my dear?"

I took the opportunity to thank him for challenging me and creating the opportunity to speak during our closing ceremony.

He looked me in the eyes, never breaking his bright, shiny grin, and placed his hand on my shoulder, "Did you notice how people responded when you were speaking? How you speak is different. You have the wisdom of experience, and share from your heart."

This observation was so simplistic, but it landed with me. It didn't matter that I wasn't polished, perfect, or comfortable with attention. What mattered was that I shared my experience authentically, from the heart because that's the source of our connection.

I thanked him and confessed, "I have grown so much here, but I do feel nervous about going home. Going back to the western world."

He tilted his head to one side and shrugged as if to express: *Why worry?*

"Tracie, when I was young, getting ready to leave my master at the ashram, I asked these same questions. Where will I go? What will I do? And my Guru said 'Only be present to this day.'"

I nodded in acknowledgement.

"The Vedas end with two words, *Neti Neti*. Do you know these words?"

I shook my head.

"This means *'neither this, nor that.'* These words guide us. If you can name it, it is not who you are. When you identify with a feeling, a person, or a place, this is not you. A teacher is a teacher whether they have a building or do not. I left the ashram with no money and no school, but I began to teach. First, just one student. Then another student. Now, I am here."

I nodded as if I understood, but really what I meant was, I hear you and will think on this.

I bowed my head, thanked him for his time, and carried his wisdom with me on my walk to town carrying the parcel I was going to ship to my son.

Indeed, I had identified with internalized feelings like *invisible*, *unworthy*, and *undeserving*. I identified with my work, relationships, status, homes, and possessions, but those are not who *I am*. Maybe if I embraced who *I am*, and stepped into my purpose, I would find that the problems and obstacles of the mind would diminish. Would feeling lack be impossible if I detached from identifying with and losing these things because they are not who *I am? I am* already whole and complete.

I had arrived at my destination, the post office. The nondescript building didn't offer a polished exterior, and inside, there was no slick presentation or any process simplified by technology. Once I crossed the threshold, I was in a space that told a story, and time seemed to slow to a crawl. The place was a mood.

It seemed the building existed prior to electricity because wires and conduit ran exposed along its interior masonry walls. The elderly postmaster invited me to take a seat and pointed to an antique, wooden chair just inside the second room. He began reinforcing my box with tape and carefully applied the necessary labels. While he was working slowly and deliberately, I soaked up the texture of the environment. Rolls of paper tied with string, stamps, sealing wax, layers of peeling and chipping buttery yellow paint, turquoise wood doors and shutters with heavy iron latches. Personally, I preferred the honesty and character of places like it to soulless, western commerce. The slowness. The sitting. The conversation. The exchange of pleasantries and cultural curiosity.

"You live in Washington? Maybe I will come visit you!"

We laughed and I told him about the bears and lions.

"Well, we have tigers and elephants! This is no problem!"

We laughed again.

The conversation with Guru Vishnu was the perfect segue. I actually enjoy character, imperfection, and experience. I see beauty in the wear and tear and the value of connection.

After I left my package in good hands, I stepped back out into the sun and noticed that the shuttered temple I had walked past nearly every day had all of its doors open. I thought the structure was long closed or abandoned, but people were entering, so I followed, covering my head with my scarf in reverence.

Inside, there was a gilded altar and to its right, in a niche, there was a goat surrounded by fruit and flowers. It was unclear if the animal was revered, sacrificial, or a future meal. Monks began chanting, beating drums, and ringing the temple bells. The cacophony of sound echoed through the interior and vibrated through my body. I have no idea why I felt called to enter, but for a moment, I enjoyed the experience which was unlike any other.

When an experience is meant for you, you will find the door open.

April 27

We had a sound healing ceremony at 5 a.m. facilitated by our classmate Mia. After the session, she informed me that while we were lying on our mats in the yoga hall, a lizard was circling me. I didn't see it because my eyes were closed.

Lizard is a symbol for outgrowing and shedding what no longer serves you. To escape danger, lizards have the ability to leave behind parts, like a leg or tail and regrow them. There's certainly a message there—sacrifice what you must in the service of regeneration.

After sound healing, meditation class began—I removed my notebook from my bag, and it was soaking wet. I'm an avid note taker, and I meticulously copied every word my Kriya instructor Praveen Rajput spoke. All of the kriyas we learned were passed down in the oral tradition. They aren't found in books. This was one of my worst fears—that I would lose my journals—that I would lose what I learned. I watched the ink bleeding into the soaked pages, which were softening. During my meditation class, I felt panicked and kept fighting the feeling. I was supposed to be meditating with everyone else, but I couldn't stop worrying about the bleeding ink. Was this a Shakti lesson in detachment? My anxiety grew, and I decided I needed to leave. I didn't ask my teacher's permission. I just gathered my belongings and went to my room, peeled the pages apart, and removed them from the spiral binding of the notebook. I placed them flat on the floor to dry. As of this evening they are salvaged. Nothing else in my bag was wet. My books were dry. My water bottle was full, and the cap was tight. My tissues were dry.

* * *

I continued my *nine days of devotion* and had a breathwork session with Tanvi, a Kundalini instructor from southern California.

The term breathwork is having a moment in the West, but it's still a mystery to the majority. Breathwork is a catchall word for a wide swath of breathing techniques such as Pranayama in India, the transcendental shamanic practices of the Americas, Africa, Australia, and New Zealand (to name a few), and modern practices such as Holotropic breathing. When used intentionally, the breath pattern can contribute to shifts in consciousness and psychedelic experiences on par with psychoactive substances.

Tanvi guided holotropic breath through three stages and asked me to imagine specific ages 17—14—6—3—1—*en utero*. She asked me to re-experience what it was like to be each age asking, "What are you wearing? What's a story in your life that has rippling effects in the future?" There was some overlap with my session with Maa Haripriya though; in this session, I was observing. There was no longer an emotional charge.

An unrelated image came to mind, one I had seen repeatedly in meditations since arriving in India. I am standing barefoot on a large rock in the river holding a large, bronze vessel filled with water. A large crow appears and says "Don't turn back." This time, the bird places a pearl in the palm of my right hand. Then I heard a woman's voice, "Your power is in your hands. You're meant to heal."

This was the same message that came through in my ceremony with the Tsáchila one year earlier, but this time, I was healed enough to hear it.

April 27
I had dinner with Narendra at Shiva Yog Stahl. We always have the best conversations. He has a very grounded spirituality I enjoy. I told him how my plans were unfolding as I prepared to return home and he said, "God has something better for you. I know you will be fine and have everything you need because God will provide it. I don't count on anything from other people. I don't expect anything from other people. I get what I am meant to have from God." I liked that idea. He said there's no need to worry about anything because "you have a purpose and as long as you are in the world doing work that serves God, you will be taken care of by the Universe."

* * *

I had reached the point in my journey where everything was the *last time*. The last time I would sit in meditation with Sunil Bisht; the last time I would be guided through kriya with Praveen

Rajput; the last Hatha instruction with Pradeep Aswal; the last time I would hear Anant Jethuri sing the *Shree Vakratunda Mahakaya* mantra at the start of our anatomy class; the last time I would visit my favorite juice bar with a friend or have dinner with my favorite hotelier.

April 28

Today was a little harder than previous days. I started to feel pretty sad mid-morning—realizing everything is now the "last" thing. The last time I'll walk to the river, the last time I'll say, "Hi" to the Sikh Chai guy; the last time I'll see my friends; the last time I'll volunteer at Prasad or spend time with Mana.

* * *

With the mantle of flowers I wore at graduation in my hand, I walked to the Ganga for the last time and stood in her water. I removed each orange flower from the strand and placed them one by one in the mystic river.

Thank you for calling me home. Thank you for showing me what I needed to heal. Thank you for guiding me back to my heart.

The orange of the marigolds in the hazy green of the water is deeply imprinted in my heart as the palette of transformation. I left a few tears in the water for good measure. But this time, they were tears of gratitude.

I followed the path along the river to find my favorite flower seller and told him that I had to return to my home.

"When are you coming back?"

"I don't know, but I hope I will see you again."

He hugged me around my waist, and I nearly fell apart. I gave him all that remained of my sweets, patted him on the head, then walked on to meet Mana.

Together with her friends and family, we spent an hour talking and cutting fresh fruit for Prasad, creating a beautiful, abundant assortment of melons and banana. We were outside, and there was magic in the air. People were happy. We were happy.

A man that I often passed along the road approached me. He was a beggar with severe conditions that resembled cerebral palsy. I gave him money on several occasions because I couldn't see any possibility that he could earn it for himself. Every time he passed me, he excitedly waved and though he was non-verbal, he attempted a greeting. It seemed terribly unfair that he had no way to communicate since his body appeared painfully crippled, and his hands were frozen in tight shapes near his chest.

I handed him a piece of watermelon, but he excitedly pointed to the banana on the tray, so I placed both in his hands which shook and jerked uncontrollably. His excitement over receiving the fruit was contagious.

He hobbled to the stone wall to sit down and eat. I watched as he tried to make his hand reach his mouth to take a bite of melon, and my heart ached to see how difficult this simple task was. He managed to get a few bites before dropping it in the dirt. I watched him struggle with the banana and realized he couldn't peel it.

That's when I heard the voice.

Take him another.

I took a banana to him and looked into his eyes. I don't know how to explain the full depth of the experience, but in front of me was a man who had been given a very difficult path in life, and he looked as though he wanted to cry because a moment ago, he was so close to enjoying the banana he was given.

I peeled the banana and then offered it to him. Instead of taking it in his shaking hands. He gestured for me to place it in his mouth.

That's when I heard the voice again.

Feed him.

C'mon. No. Not that.

Feed him.

This was my *really real* graduation.

My channel was clear. I was listening. Would I serve?

I broke off a piece of banana and held it up to his mouth. He opened his mouth wide, and I fed him. By the grace of God, I fed him. And I felt all of the love in the Universe flow through me in that moment. I realized how much I have. My blessings. My fortune. My health. My ability to serve.

After he finished eating, he got up from the wall and began to move in big circles like he was racing. Then he began howling in joy with his mouth open wide towards the heavens. This was the joy of tasting a banana. To my ears, it was a sacred song I will never forget. It had no words, only the sounds of praise he could muster from his languageless throat, but I understood what he was saying. He was thanking God, and I was humbled to have been called to service in this way. I was the one who had been given the gift of Prasad, not him.

In that moment, I understood the message of the Bhagavad Gita. The spiritual seeker has a duty (dharma) which must be fulfilled through acts of devotion (Bhakti yoga) and selfless action (Karma yoga) to achieve liberation (Moksha) from the cycle of life and death and know the ultimate truth.

What is that ultimate truth? We are here to open our hearts wide. We are meant to share our abundance because in the sharing we receive more than we give, and the Universe reciprocates with *more*. We are meant to let the energy of compassion and care work through us. We are vessels for the Divine.

I felt so moved and it was such a tender day. Not long after witnessing this Divine joy, I hugged Mana and we said our goodbyes, but I knew I would see her again. Maybe not in this lifetime, but I would see her.

I returned to the ashram, said goodbye to my friends, packed my bags, and settled in for the night. I had forty hours of travel ahead of me and needed rest, but I couldn't relax. I was wide awake and alert. My body was buzzing with energy, and I felt restless. It was nearly nine o'clock in the evening, and the gates would be locked at ten, but I felt pulled to the river. So, I decided to walk the path one more time.

When I reached the dirt road in front of the ashram, it was especially dark. I stood there for a moment wondering where I was going to begin; then, I heard, "Oh, hey, where are you off to?" I looked across the path and it was New Zealand Charley looking handsome as ever in his signature barely buttoned oxford shirt with rolled sleeves, the perfect contrast to his wild curls.

Just as I started to cross the road towards him, I heard a scooter racing towards us and its headlight was a bit blinding. I stepped backwards to let it pass, but it came to an abrupt halt between Charley and me.

It was Guru Vishnu. *He has a scooter?*

He looked at me and asked, "Where are you going?"

"I don't know."

"OK. I will give you a ride."

Is this real?

The whole thing felt ridiculous—a Guru on a scooter giving me a ride to *I don't know*. I didn't even think about it. I got on, careful not to touch him because that seems like the kind of thing that would be taboo. I tucked my fingers under the back of the seat to steady myself and off we went.

He said, "I am going to Tapovan. Where would you like to go?"

"You can drop me off at the Ram Jhula Bridge on your way, and I will walk back from there."

The stars were sparkling in the black, night sky. The air was cool and refreshing. His long hair occasionally reached my cheeks and smelled like a temple.

"Where do you live in the United States, Tracie?"

"I live in the mountains of Washington state."

"I would like to visit the United States someday."

"Maybe I will plan a retreat for you!" I said.

"You are so nice. You have a peaceful energy."

I agreed with him because I did have peaceful energy. I was at peace.

Guru dropped me off near the bridge, and as he drove away, I stood there at the end of our story, which was really just the beginning.

I didn't know what would happen next, but I took my first step.

नेति नेति

Neti Neti

www.ingramcontent.com/pod-product-compliance
Lightning Source LLC
Chambersburg PA
CBHW030821090426
42737CB00009B/819